The Book of Bulla

Manjul Bajaj graduated in Economics followed by masters degrees in Rural Management and Environmental Science. She worked as a development and environment professional for many years before becoming an author. Her debut novel, *Come, Before Evening Falls*, was shortlisted for The Hindu Literary Prize 2010 and her collection of short stories, *Another Man's Wife*, was shortlisted for The Hindu Literary Prize 2013. Her novel *In Search of Heer* was listed for several prizes, including the JCB Prize for Literature in 2020. She is also the author of *Elbie's Quest* and *Nargisa's Adventures*, two books for children. She lives in Goa with her husband.

THE BOOK OF
BULLAH

A Selection of Verses

Manjul Bajaj

AMARYLLIS

An imprint of Manjul Publishing House Pvt. Ltd.
• C-16, Sector 3, Noida, Uttar Pradesh 201301, India
Website: www.manjulindia.com

Registered Office:
• 10, Nishat Colony, Bhopal 462 003 – India

Distribution Centres
Ahmedabad, Bengaluru, Bhopal, Chennai, Hyderabad,
Kolkata, Mumbai, Noida, Pune

The Book of Bullah by Manjul Bajaj

Copyright © Manjul Bajaj, 2024
All Rights Reserved

Manjul Bajaj asserts the moral right to be identified
as the author of this work

This paperback edition first published in India in 2024

ISBN 978-93-5543-830-0

Cover design and inside illustrations: Danette Gomes

Printed and bound in India by Parksons Graphics Pvt. Ltd.

The interpretation of the verses of Bulleh Shah is the author's own,
and the publishers are not in any way liable for the same.

The objective of this book is not to hurt any sentiments or be
biased in favour of or against any particular person, political party,
region, caste, society, gender, creed, nation or religion.

All rights reserved. No part of this book may be used or reproduced,
stored in or introduced into a retrieval system, or transmitted, in any form, or
by any means (electronic, mechanical, photocopying, recording or otherwise)
without the prior written permission of the Author. Any person who does any
unauthorized act in relation to this publication may be liable to
criminal prosecution and civil claims for damages.

Contents

Preface ix

1. Come, Bullah — 1
2. Bullah, How Do I Know — 3
3. Neither Hindu nor Muslim — 7
4. A Is for Allah — 9
5. I Am Lost — 13
6. I Am Free — 15
7. What Happened to Me — 17
8. The Sound of the Flute — 19
9. The Lover's Style — 21
10. Look What He Has Done — 25
11. They Come to Reason with Bullah — 27
12. Only You — 30
13. The Noise No Longer Pleases — 31
14. On Love's Swings — 35
15. To the Beloved's Country — 37
16. Fasts, Pilgrimages, Prayers — 41
17. Toss the Prayers — 43
18. Who Shall See God — 45
19. Happiness — 47
20. The Hawkers Are Here — 49
21. Sack the Timekeeper — 52
22. Love Blossoms Ever New — 53

23. Calling to the Beloved	57
24. I Meditate on Your Name	58
25. Ego	61
26. Who Will Recognise Me	62
27. In the Grip of Love	65
28. I Have Found Something	67
29. The Beloved Has Come as a Man	69
30. Clay	73
31. Fate	75
32. Separation	77
33. Let's Go to the Lover's Kitchen	78
34. The Lover Has Left	79
35. Turn Your Head Towards Us	81
36. Let Me Merge	83
37. What's to Be Done	87
38. Waiting for Him	89
39. By the Riverbank	91
40. O Traveller	95
41. I'm in Love	97
42. My Heart Is Yearning	98
43. Heartless One	101
44. I Write to Shyam	103
45. Don't Act Coy	106
46. Stop It Now	108
47. A Spell	111
48. In Love I Dance	113
49. Come, Meet Me	117
50. Ranjha Is All I Need	120

51. Ranjha! Ranjha! I Call	122
52. Congratulate Me, Friends	125
53. I Am Crazy	128
54. Ranjha Has Come as a Jogi	131
55. Why Should I Go to Ka'aba	133
56. The Good Days	137
57. Gathering Safflowers	138
58. The Spinning Wheel Is Broken	141
59. Sisters, I Am Tired of Spinning	143
60. Spin, Don't Be Idle	147
61. Gold	149
62. Gather Around Me, Precious Girlfriends	150
63. Cotton	153
64. Khaki	155
65. Live Quietly	159
66. Make the Ganga Flow Backwards	161
67. Sweeper	163
68. Keep Away	165
69. The Only Place	167
70. With This Knowledge I'm Ablaze	169
71. Finding God	171
72. Eat What Is Forbidden	172
73. Drink Wine	173
74. Say Yes	174
75. People Tell Bullah	175
76. If God Came to the Temple	176
77. The Thief	177
78. Be Done with Learning	181

79. A Simple Truth Ends the Matter	183
80. The Matter Doesn't End	187
81. Go Beyond Reading	189
82. From the Half-Learned I Flee	190
83. Hats Off 1	191
84. Hats Off 2	192
85. Don't Pray for Forgiveness	193
86. Where Do You Come From	197
87. Your God Is Distant	199
88. The Times Are Perverse	201
89. The Play of Clay	203
90. Dogs Do Better	205
91. Unless We Experience Love	207
92. Wake Up, Traveller	209
93. That Friend	211
94. God Is Light	212
95. Play in the Courtyard	213
96. Let's Go and See	217
97. River of Unity	219
98. Let's Go to the Fair	223
99. You	225
100. Who	227
Index of Punjabi Poems	228
Bibliography	232
Acknowledgements	234

Preface

This volume of Bulleh Shah's poetry, rendered in English by me, comes to you from a space of great love and very sincere endeavour. I am no scholar or authority on Punjabi poetry, and this is not meant as a scholarly offering. It is an attempt to share with non-Punjabi-speaking readers (as well as those who are conversant with spoken Punjabi but cannot navigate the literature with ease) a glimpse into the incredible emotional range, profound wisdom and sheer beauty of the work of this mystic poet born in the late seventeenth century. Centuries later, Bulleh Shah continues to be a dominant voice and pervasive influence on the artistic and cultural landscape of Punjab, on either side of the Indo-Pak border, his work inspiring fresh interpretations and garnering new enthusiasts and converts as time passes.

Bulleh Shah: Life and Times

While precise dates are not available, Bulleh Shah is widely believed to have lived from 1680 to 1758. The chief source of biographical information about him is what can be gleaned from his own poetry and from anecdotes about his life circulating in oral lore. Bullah was the childhood name, and later nom de plume, of Abdullah Shah, born to a pious Syed family near Bahawalpur in south-west Punjab. His father was a learned Islamic scholar and Bullah received an orthodox religious education in Qasur. It is evident from his own work that in addition to Punjabi, Bullah had studied Arabic and Persian and was well-versed in the Quran, Islamic law and Persian literature.

In his youth, he rebelled against conventional religion and became a disciple of Shah Inayat Qadri of Lahore, a cultivator by caste and gardener by profession, but also a renowned Sufi scholar of the Qadri order and author of several books on mysticism. This caused consternation in Bullah's high-caste Syed family, but he remained obdurate in his devotion to his Master. One of the more important incidents in Bulleh Shah's life was an estrangement from his Master, which resulted in his being thrown out of the Master's camp. This led to a period of intense grief and half-crazed torment for Bullah and forms the subject of many of his poems. The later rapprochement, achieved by Bullah breaking into the Master's presence disguised as a dancing girl, is the subject of one of his most ecstatic and popular verses: '*Tere Ishq Nachaiyan.*'

Shah Inayat passed away in 1728 and Bulleh Shah continued his work as a teacher and poet with the Qadri order, finally retiring to Qasur in his last years. His later poetry reflects the concerns of a spiritual guide urging his followers to a better understanding of life and death, truth, morality and faith. The Punjab of his later years was a land of great political upheaval and strife. The Mughal Empire was on the decline, petty dictators and tyrants tormented the common people, Sikhism was coming up in the region accompanied by great cruelty and repression from the Muslim rulers, and a series of invasions by Nadir Shah and Ahmad Shah Abdali had brought the region to its knees, its spirit broken. This political reality also forms the subject matter of his poetry, reflecting both despair at the state of affairs and scorn for the political masters in equal measure.

Throughout his life, Bulleh Shah remained an iconoclast and fierce critic of established religion. Preaching against intolerance and the entrenched dogmas of the various faiths and the rigid observance of rituals formed a large part of Bulleh Shah's message.

Upon his death, he was refused burial at the mosque by the clerics in Qasur. Ironically, Bulleh Shah's tomb in Qasur is today its most distinguished grave, burial in its vicinity a privilege sought out by the city's elite.

Punjab: Its Language and Its Literature

Bulleh Shah belongs firmly inside the oral troubadour tradition of Punjab. It is important to understand the centrality of Sufi poetry and music to the development of the Punjabi language as we know it today. The earliest extant record of Punjabi literature begins with Bulleh Shah's thirteenth-century predecessor, the Sufi saint Baba Farid. Punjab, while being home to the one of the world's earliest recorded civilisations in the Indus Valley and famed for the historic Takshila University of seventh century BCE, has very scant surviving literature from earlier times. A likely theory is that manuscripts predating this were destroyed in the many invasions witnessed by this land over the centuries from Alexander the Great to the Huns and to the invasions of Mahmud of Ghazni and Muhammad Ghori.

The literary language of the Punjab of the seventh to tenth centuries was *Natha Bhasha*, an archaic version of Prakrit Punjabi in which the poetry of the Nath jogis was written. With the advent of Sufism that followed in the wake of the Ghaznavid rule, the local Prakrit language combined with Persian influences, and Shahmukhi, which is based on the Perso-Arabic script, began to be used to write Punjabi. Later, the Sikh gurus developed and popularised the Gurmukhi alphabet (from the original vowel-less Lendi script of the trader community), and the language attained its primarily biscriptal character which it retains till today. It is additionally written in the Devanagari script. It is evident that Bulleh Shah wrote his verses in Shahmukhi, from the frequent referencing of the Urdu alphabet in his verses.

For the next four centuries following Baba Farid, the Sufi kafis and Sikh shabads were the primary engine driving the language, mixing poetic elements from the east and west, Brajbhasha and Persian, with the folk idiom and day-to-day language of common people. Elements of Sufism, Sikhism and the Bhakti movement (from the neighbouring regions) came together in shaping the language. Baba Farid's songs were included by Guru Nanak in the Guru Granth Sahib as were those of Kabir. Among the many Sufi poets after Baba Farid and preceding Bulleh Shah, the most significant names are those of Shah Hussain and Sultan Bahu. These earlier poets used the many dialects of Punjab for their verses. It is with Bulleh Shah and his contemporary Waris Shah that Maajhi or central Punjabi came to be established as the dominant or standard literary language of Punjab. Coincidently, both Bulleh Shah and Waris Shah are believed to be students of the same teacher in Qasur, although at different times.

The Kafi as a Poetic Form

The kafi, a form central to the poetry of Punjab, stands at the intersection of poetry and music. It was written not to be read, but to be conveyed via a singing voice, the singer's emphasis, pauses and nuances of voice adding a layer of meaning. It is typically performed by a group of singers and listened to by an involved audience. There is some difference between scholars whether the word kafi evolved from the Persian word *kafiya* (rhyme) or the Arabic word *kafa* (group). Be that as it may, the kafi is a poem of several stanzas, opened with and followed by a refrain, sung to folk or classical music, by a group of qawwals. The music is strophic, that is, successive stanzas are sung to the same tune and they build in intensity and rhythm over the performance. The refrain is a key element of the kafi, establishing a certain dialogue and intimacy with the listener before leading him into the heart of the composition.

The Conventions of Sufi Poetry

Here, I would like to put before the reader some of the key elements of Punjabi Sufi poetry in general and Bulleh Shah's style in particular. A few minutes spent in understanding the conventions of this poetry will enable the reader to appreciate it better. Many of the kafis are vocative, that is, the opening line is addressed to someone. The poet variously invokes a lover, a mother, girlfriends, fellow travellers, or others to whom the poem is being said, in the voice of the persona the poet has donned for that piece. This is an element of folk songs that was possibly adopted by the Sufis to draw the common people into their gatherings.

Another convention of Sufi poetry is that the poet often addresses himself in the poem, typically in the final stanza, but often also in the refrain. Additionally, following the style of devotional poetry across South Asia, Bulleh Shah assumes a female persona and alludes to God or his Master as the male beloved. In the Sufi and Bhakti traditions, God is thought of as male, and the seeker, regardless of actual gender, is represented as female.

A third element, not used by his predecessors in Punjab but a much-used element in Bulleh Shah's poetry, is to reference the poet's master, Shah Inayat Qadri, either by name or as the beloved or Master. An intensely personal engagement with the Master which rips past the defences of the follower and leaves him naked and exposed is integral to the Sufi tradition. The *murshid–murid* or master–disciple relationship is tumultuous, emotionally charged, multi-layered and passionate. It follows no rules, as it is a no-holds-barred experience of love that dissolves the follower's ego, breaks the barriers of social conditioning and held beliefs and takes him past received wisdom into a direct knowing and oneness with creation. Readers might be familiar with this from the style of Rumi's ghazals and his referencing of Shams Tabrizi.

Bulleh Shah: Literary Influences

The famed thirteenth-century Persian poet Rumi's poetry is believed to be one of the influences on Bulleh Shah's writing. One of Bulleh Shah's most iconic verses, *'Bulla Ki Jaana Main Kaun'*, is a close translation from a ghazal in Rumi's *Diwan-e-Shams Tabriz*. However, Bulleh Shah's poetry largely follows a language and aesthetic sensibility which is more home-spun and rooted in the milieu of rural Punjab. The beloved, the beloved's beauty, wine, the cupbearer and the tavern, the motifs that Persian Sufi poetry revolves around find less frequent mention in Bulleh Shah's work. The images are instead drawn from social customs, kinship relations, farming practices, the domestic cotton industry, journeys by boat or through the wilderness and from the popular love stories of the region like Heer–Ranjha and Sassi–Pannu. Also visible are the influences of Kabir and the bhakti poets in verses that address Krishna and allude to stories from Hindu mythology.

Bulleh Shah: Metaphors, Motifs and Symbols

Let us explore a bit further the cultural emblems, symbols and motifs that pervade Bulleh Shah's poetry. The image of the young girl on the eve of her marriage is one of the major symbols in Bulleh Shah's poetry. Another pervasive symbol is that of the spinning wheel. The spinning wheel represents human endeavour, the deeds performed during the course of a life, while the soul is represented by the young girl required to prepare her dowry before her wedding day. The dowry here is a reference to the accumulation of good karma and the wedding day is the day of death, the day when the bride of life will marry the bridegroom of death. Depending on the context of the poem, the bridegroom can be interpreted as a stand-in for God or for Death. Another set of metaphors along these lines are the allusions to the parents' home and the in-laws' place, the former referring to the familiar comforts of everyday life on earth, the latter to the unknown future that is the afterlife of the soul.

It is important to understand these symbols but even more important not to get lost in them or give them primacy. The poem must work first at the level of lived experience, at the level of everyday reality and felt emotion before it can illuminate any greater truths. In my opinion, Bulleh Shah's intent was not to impart obtuse mystical lessons to his listeners but to engage with them through their feelings, take them into the conflicts and issues in their own lives, arouse them and provoke them, and then gently leave them at a place where they might come to a questioning of the deeper meaning of life. In the same way, while in the passionately expressed longing for the beloved it is God who is being referred to, the poet is deliberately taking the listener into their own experience of earthly love, its anxieties and its ecstasy. In this way he signals that all love is essentially divine, that the knowing of love is what the knowing of God can be anticipated to feel like. He leads the listener into the unknown via the known, his fingers on the emotional pulse of his audience.

The state of *virah* or separation is the central motif of many of Bulleh Shah's songs. Deep yearning or intense longing can only be experienced by the absence of the loved one. Love defines itself as much by the throes of the pain that is suffered for its lack as by the bliss of union. The dark night of the soul is mandatory before the light can be seen in all its glory. Bulleh Shah went through a period of estrangement from his master and some of his most intense poems were written in this phase of his discipleship.

Another metaphor central to the poetry is the love story of Heer and Ranjha (and also Sassi–Pannu). This folktale is so embedded in the psyche of Punjab that a mere mention of the names associated with the tale will set off a whole series of associations and understandings for the listener for whom the backstory is always familiar, a compass for navigating the vicissitudes of life. In the Sufi universe, Heer is the longing of the soul for union with God, while Ranjha is the divine beloved. The Kheras, Heer's in-laws, represent the demands of conventional life, while allusions to Mecca refer to the dictates of formal religion. The reader will find numerous references to Takht Hazara, Ranjha's birthplace. It represents the mystic idyll, the place where union between the soul and the divine spirit pervading the universe is achieved. The mystic, when he reaches his goal, knows it as pure ecstasy in which the sense of self ceases to exist.

Yet another set of symbols frequently present in the poetry revolve around day and night, travelling and wandering, encountering the wilderness and savage beasts and around boats and waiting for the ferry to be taken across the river. The exact connotation of these symbols will depend on the context of the poem. The wanderer or fakir alludes to the soul which is passing through this world for a limited time, its days on earth finite. The fair or mela refer to the transient pleasures of the world. Light or day signify the bliss of union and the dark or night the grief of separation. The wilderness and beasts signify the turbulence of life, the anxieties, uncertainties and fears that loom large and cast shadows on man's life on earth. The river that needs crossing is the river of duality, and in Bulleh Shah's universe the Master helms the boat that can take the soul across this vast divide, from unknowing into enlightenment. *Wahdat-ul-wajud* is a key Sufi concept meaning the unity of existence or the oneness of being, its realisation the soul's ultimate goal.

Bulleh Shah: Poetic Style and Themes

One of the distinguishing features of Bulleh Shah's kafis and perhaps one of the main reasons behind the raging popularity, enduring appeal and memorability of his verses is the way in which he framed the refrains of his verses. The language used is non-poetic, blunt, drawn from everyday conversations, full of spontaneity and gusto: a mother scolds a daughter for idling; a daughter tells her mother not to stop her as she runs after her lover; a bride asks her girlfriends to surround her on the eve of her departure to the husband's home; a woman accuses her lover of heartlessness; Heer declares herself crazy; the poet urges believers to smash mosques and topple temples; he claims to be a sweeper; shouts impatiently at scholars to be done with learning; scornfully claims dogs are better at worshipping than people. The refrain aims to grab the listener's attention, intrigue, or provoke him, draw out sighs of recognition and instant applause. These simple, dramatic openings then preface the verses which in themselves are rhyming and complex in meaning. Najm Hossain Syed puts it perfectly when he writes that 'A Bulleh Shah kafi is a miniature drama in which diverse, contrasting notes converge to create the final meaning.'

In Bulleh Shah's verse we find the straightforward and the spiritual combining seamlessly. Such is the expanse and range of themes that his poetry deals with, that Islamic scholars, believers in Advaita philosophy, Vaishnav worshippers, as well as sceptics of religion, rebels and free thinkers of different persuasions all claim that he speaks for them. As indeed he does, for his is a transcendental outlook, rising above human differences and speaking directly of and to the human spirit. In essence, Bulleh Shah is a lover of unity and oneness, and his love bows at every threshold.

Bulleh Shah: In Popular Culture

My first brush with Bulleh Shah came when I was young child watching the 1973 blockbuster film *Bobby* in a dark, rat-infested, second-rate cinema hall in Bareilly in Uttar Pradesh, where my mother and I had gone to spend the winter holidays with my uncle's family. It was an exceptionally cold December evening, the seats in the hall were movable, and there were the disconcerting sounds of chairs scraping and mice scurrying on the floor. And then Narinder Chanchal's piercing, high-pitched voice rang out *'Beshak mandir masjid dha de, weh Bulleh Shah eh kainda'* and filled the hall with a collective gasp and then an eerie stillness. I'm not sure how much I understood the song's message back then, but it left a lasting impression of something mystical and other-worldly. Of Bulleh Shah as someone to be heard with awe. The next conscious coming face to face with his poetry happened decades later in 2004 with Rabbi Shergill's inspired rendering of *'Bulla Ki Jaana Main Kaun'*.

After that I sought Bullah and found him everywhere in the repertoire of qawwals and in popular culture. Nusrat Fateh Ali Khan, Abida Parveen, the Wadali brothers, Pathanay Khan, the rock band Junoon, Coke Studio and film songs to name only a few – there was such a wealth of music based on Bulleh Shah's kafis that it felt inconceivable that a single man was behind it all. From songs of ecstatic love and celebration to songs of unrequited love and heartbreak, to existential probing, to didactic, admonishing songs of warnings to followers to be virtuous, to songs of rebellion and rage against the clerics and the establishment, to songs of despair and sadness about the political situation – Bulleh Shah had written them all.

I would have been content to remain an enthusiastic listener, but fate had other plans for me. At a visit to an older friend's home, I came across the Hind Pocket Books' bilingual volume of Bulleh Shah's poems by Dr Harbhajan Singh and Dr Shoaib Nadvi – in Devanagari script alongside the Shahmukhi. The authors had also included a short prose commentary on each piece in Hindi. I borrowed the volume with great excitement. My friend and I discussed some of the pieces over the phone and when I shared with her the thought that I'd like to render a few of the poems in English, she generously told me I could keep the book for as long as I liked. I don't think she meant forever, but that is how it turned out to be.

I began work on this volume in 2013, but for reasons I'm not entirely sure about, it was abandoned at the halfway mark. I had fifty kafis in translation that I meant to publish someday. I returned to them many times in the last ten years, to read them, to find joy and resonance in them, to remind myself that I needed to complete this project. However, it was only in 2023 that I began once again. I brought a ten-years-older self to the project, as a consequence of which the work before you is better researched and more informed. I consulted as much of the published literature on Bulleh Shah as I could find, familiarised myself with other English translations of his work, took time to crosscheck the different versions of the same poem in Shahmukhi and Gurmukhi (in itself no mean task as I cannot read either script and had to rely on Devanagari to access the material) and compared how the written corpus differs from the oral tradition.

It was with some chagrin that I discovered that the verified poems attributed to Bulleh Shah in the published literature are at some variance with what is attributed to him in the Qawwali tradition. I searched for the '*Main Ni Bolna*' song from *Bobby* that had first captured my heart but could not find its exact counterpart in the 160-odd kafis attributed to Bulleh Shah in the different compilations, though the central thought and style seem to belong there. Another favourite kafi frequently attributed to him, '*Mahiya Tere Vekhan Nu*', also did not make its way into this volume as deeper probing seems to suggest that it belongs to Baba Farid's oeuvre. Yet another disappointment was not being able to present to the reader Abida Parveen's '*Assa Ishq Namaz Jado Neeti Hai*' in the form it appears in the Qawwali tradition. The different stanzas are taken from across his poems and dohas and strung together to form this beautiful qawwali. The reason for these discrepancies is that his work was not recorded till almost a century and a half after his death.

It is to the qawwals who performed his work in an unbroken tradition that we owe the preservation and survival of Bulleh Shah's work. But the Qawwali tradition is a living, ever-adapting, dynamic tradition, and the qawwals interpreted his writing to the needs of their audiences, adding and subtracting stanzas, switching phrases from one dialect to another, stringing different pieces together, thus corrupting the original. It was only after the emergence of the publishing industry in Lahore in the mid-nineteenth century that written compilations of Bulleh Shah's work were made and brought out based on what different scholars writing in Shahmukhi and Gurmukhi could collate from folk sources. The earliest substantial edition of his work was published in 1889 and contained 117 kafis. The current literature recognises about 160 kafis and 55 dohre as belonging to Bulleh Shah with certainty. In addition, there are more stylised poems like the *Barahmasa* which is based on the twelve months of the year, the *Athwaria* based on the seven days of the week, *Gandian* based on the local practice of tying knots to do a countdown to the wedding day and *Siharfi* or acrostic poem based on the alphabet.

Notes on This Translation

For the purpose of this volume, I have restricted myself to the kafis and the dohre, leaving out the more stylised compositions which do not travel well from Punjabi to English. While I have followed what is available in the textual literature for the pieces included in this volume for reasons of consistency, I do believe that the oral sources offer an incomparable, authentic experiencing of the poet's essence and intent. To my mind, like the qawwali which is sung by multiple singers following the lead performer, a Bulleh Shah kafi also comes to us in the same nuanced, collective voice with one dominant singer and a chorus of other voices that blend in.

In bringing this volume to you I wanted to create an immersive experience for the reader. In most of the editions I consulted, the work is presented in alphabetical order by opening lines. This is frequently jarring and takes away from the reading experience as poems with different themes and from different phases of his life follow each other with no rationale. I have chosen an ordering of the pieces which is more organic and intuitive and veers towards a loose grouping of similar poems and a progression of themes.

Another departure from the norm is that the original kafi in Gurmukhi/Shahmukhi/Devanagari/Roman script is not given alongside the English translation. The reader who does not know Punjabi will not have to battle with the sense of being shut out and will instead be free to soak into the meditative space created by the illustrations. The reader who does know the language can always delve into the originals in her own time. The experience of reading the two versions alongside each other will, to my mind, take away more from the enjoyment of this book than it can possibly give. As my wise young son frequently tells me, comparison is the thief of joy. For the moment, I would urge my readers to stay inside the English rendering of each piece. There is a key in Roman script at the end which will enable you to connect the opening line of the original with the poems in this selection. There is also a bibliography provided for those who wish to read further and ample material on the internet to begin a deeper exploration of the work of this truly great poet.

My approach to this work has been to try and stay out of the conversation between Bulleh Shah and his readers in English. I have tried to stick as close as possible, within the constraints of travelling across two vastly different language sensibilities, to the intent, emotions and imagery of his poetry. I have not added in embellishments, images, or thoughts to explain it in the modern reader's context. However, in a work of mystic poetry written a few centuries ago such as this one, it is near impossible for the translator to absent themselves entirely from the translation. The poems are multi-layered and complex in meaning, and what my rendering brings to you cannot but be influenced by my own understanding of his spiritual message. Some of the kafis in his repertoire have Arabic/Persian phrases and Islamic concepts which I do not understand well enough to give you a meaningful rendering. The reader will find these poems missing in my selection. Out of the 210 kafis and dohre Bulleh Shah is credited with, this volume contains 100. So, in a sense, the act of selection itself introduces a bias.

Also, I have sacrificed to a great extent the rhyming character of his poetry in the interest of lucidity and flow. Punjabi and English are very inequitably endowed with rhyming potential, the former being far richer in this regard. In the matter of rhyming, I took the middle path – those pieces which lent themselves to rhyming with ease, and without a distortion of the meaning and nuances of the piece, have been rendered in rhyme or partial rhyme. The others are written in free verse.

In the end, I'd like to quote A.K. Ramanujan in his Translator's Note to *Poems of Love and War*:

> Even one's own tradition is not one's birthright. It has to be earned, repossessed. The old bards earned

it by apprenticing themselves to the masters. One chooses and translates a part of one's past to make it present to oneself and maybe to others.

I began this work primarily as a gift to myself. It has given me great joy and much illumination. The beauty of this gift to myself is that it does not have to be mine alone.

So here it is, dear readers, from me to you, with great love.

.1.

Come, Bullah

Come, Bullah, let us head to the place where all are blind
No one questions our caste, no one praises us – no differences of any kind

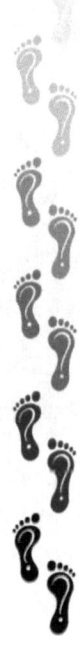

.2.

Bullah, How Do I Know

Bullah, how do I know
who I am?

I am not a believer among believers
Nor am I a disbeliever
Neither pure nor unclean
Neither Moses nor Pharaoh

Bullah, how do I know
who I am?

I am not in the Vedas or scriptures
Nor in alcohol or drugs
I'm not a drunkard or a repentant
Not asleep nor awake

Bullah, how do I know
who I am?

Neither saint nor sinner
Neither happy nor unhappy
Neither fire nor water
Neither earth nor wind

Bullah, how do I know
who I am?

Not an Arab or a Lahori
Nor do I belong to Nagori
Not a Hindu, not a Turk
Nor a dweller of Nadaun

Bullah, how do I know
who I am?

I do not know the secret of religions
I was not born of Adam and Eve
I am without a name
Without faith or disbelief

Bullah, how do I know
who I am?

I know only myself
Nothing other than the Self
Nothing greater than the Self
Who then is that I see watching me?

.3.

Neither Hindu nor Muslim

You're not Hindu, not Muslim
Come sit at the wheel
and spin
Shed that pride

The soul isn't Hindu or Muslim
Not a Shia or a Sunni

Not starving nor replete
Neither naked nor dressed

Not crying nor laughing
Belonging nowhere but not homeless

Not a sinner nor a saint
It knows no path

Bulleh Shah, when the soul
immerses itself in God
it forgets the difference
between Hindu and Turk

You're not Hindu, not Muslim
Come sit at the wheel
and spin
Shed that pride

.4.

A Is for Allah

A is for Allah
The only letter of the alphabet
That you will need

That A becomes two, three, four
Then thousands, lakhs, crores
Then on to infinity
That A is unique

Why read wagons of books?
Why carry strange loads?
They darken your face
They obscure your road

Hafiz memorised the Quran
It purified his speech
Yet, he roamed restless
His mind ensnared

Bullah, the world is a tree
grown from a single seed
It will be destroyed
Only the seed remain

A is for Allah
All the alphabet you need
Just A can set you free

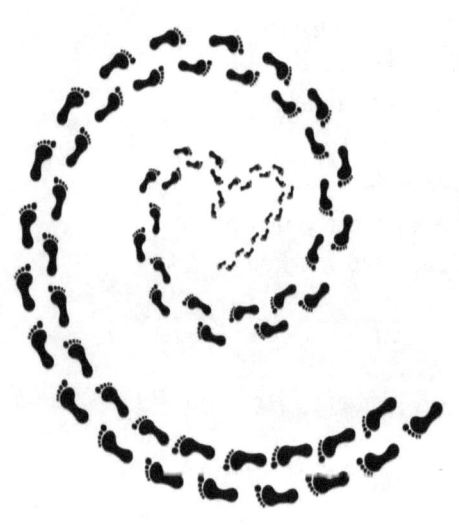

.5.

I Am Lost

I am lost, I am lost
in the city of love

I search for myself
No legs, no hands, no head
do I find
as I wander homeless

In losing myself
I have found bliss
Everyone seems my own
in this world and the next

I am lost, I am lost
in the city of love

.6.

I Am Free

I am free, I am free
Neither the healer nor diseased

Neither a believer nor in disbelief
Neither a Sayyid nor a Sa'id

Unfettered I roam
all fourteen layers of existence

Joy is my nature
I heed not praise or blame

Bullah, don't ask who God is
He is in all that is created
and in all that is unborn

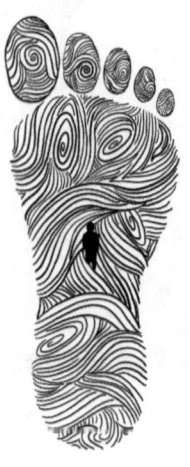

.7.

What Happened to Me

What has happened to me?
Why do they call me crazy?
I have lost the I in me

When I look inside me
all I see is you
I have lost the I in me

From head to foot
only you
I have lost the I in me

There are no banks
to this river
I have lost the I in me

No need for a boat
I have become the ocean
I have lost the I in me

Mansur said, 'I am God'
Who made him say it?
I have lost the I in me

Bulleh Shah, God loves those
who lose their ego
I have lost the I in me

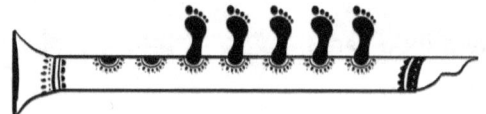

.8.

The Sound of the Flute

The flute begins to play mysteriously
Hearing it I forget all else

Struck by the celestial music
I abandon the world's false ways
Gypsies behold the Lord's face
I forget all else

Trapped like a restless deer
I become still eventually
I offer him half-done prayers
I forget all else

Bullah has been searching for his Master
Since when the first note
flowed out of Kanha's flute
Which direction should he go?

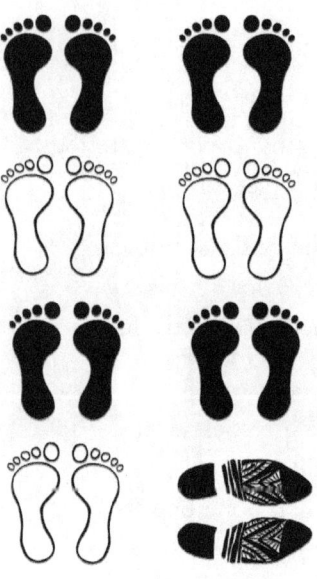

.9.

The Lover's Style

The lover's style is different
Only a lover can understand it

Let me run to the rooftops
and give out a warning call
If you fall in love, you'll find no peace
either at home or in the forest

Lovers are at risk in both worlds
slain by their beloved's airs
Love re-opens old wounds
No hope of healing

Ever since I set my eyes on him
I walk with a noose around my neck
I was careless and got robbed
by that thief of Lahore

Shirin wept in separation
Farhad was alone on the mountain
Joseph got sold in Egypt's bazaars
None recognised him there

Laila and Majnu, both were held
Shirin drowned mid-stream
Heer left her family behind
pulled along on her lover's string

Lovers roam the streets bereft
Their eyes in a drunken stupor
Ensnared in the beloved's locks
They are helpless creatures

If I find my lover
I will give up my life
He's as beautiful as Joseph
He has the world in thrall

Don't look for Bullah any more
You will not find him
The lover has neither colour nor form
Nevertheless, the lover is everywhere

The lover's style is different
Only a lover can understand it

.10.

Look What He Has Done

See what the lover has done
He has taken my heart and left

Mother scolds me, Father is livid
My brothers are full of taunts
God is my witness
One laugh and I was besotted

He came to the door, sounded the horn
and I lost my mind, my head
I could do anything, go any length
to be with him now

Bulleh Shah, this love
is worse than a snake bite
It may look as if it just happened
but this love is older than time

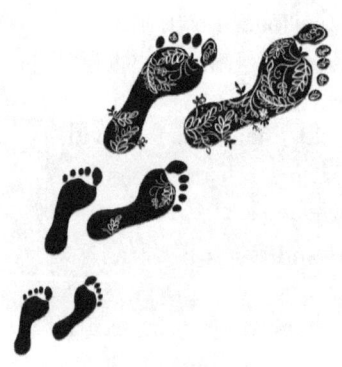

They Come to Reason with Bullah

The women of the family come
to reason with Bullah

Listen to us, Bullah, they say
Leave that farmer's side, we pray
Why should a descendant of Nabi and Ali
attach himself to a Master so lowly?

The women of the family come
to reason with Bullah

Don't call me a Sayyid now, Bullah says
Else in hell you'll spend your days
If heaven's gates you wish to get past
know me by my Master's caste

The women of the family come
to reason with Bullah

If you wish to get to heaven faster
come and serve my farmer master
What caste can you call mine
when Bullah is one with the Divine?

.12.

Only You

There is only you now, my love
Nothing remains of me

Like shadows in the ruins
you loom all around
When I speak you speak
When I'm silent it's your quiet
When I sleep you sleep with me
When I walk you walk alongside

Bullah, the husband is home
My life revolves around him

.13.

The Noise No Longer Pleases

Dear girls, noise no longer pleases me
My heart seeks contentment

A new blossom is flowering
The heart seeks a different spring
Don't say anything to me
Dear girls, the noise is no longer pleasing

Mother, I am dead now
The crow snatched my string
I ran after him begging
But he's not returning it
Dear girls, the noise is no longer pleasing

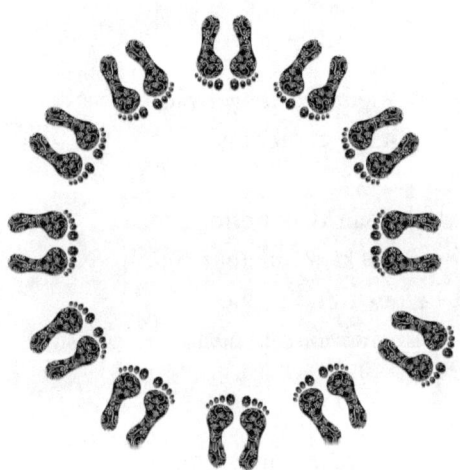

Bullah is in love with his Master
who bestows on him myriad blessings
To be near him, to be one with him
That is my decision, my choosing
Dear girls, the noise is no longer pleasing

.14.

On Love's Swings

On love's swings I soar
The friend whom I talk about
is calling me

Why do you wish to know my origins?
I belong to Adam's tribe
I live in proximity to God
In fact, he lives right inside

On love's swings I soar
The friend whom I talk about
is calling me

Some are Shia, some are Sunni
Some of matted locks, some clean-shaven
My being is free of all this
God listens to me directly

On love's swings I soar
The friend whom I talk about
is calling me

Bullah, he came from afar
His face was dazzling
He revealed his pure beauty
With every breath I remember him

On love's swings I soar
The friend whom I talk about
is calling me

.15.

To the Beloved's Country

True love destroyed me, girl
To the beloved's country show me the way

An innocent in my parents' home
Oh! How I was ruined by love!

To the beloved's country show me the way

I studied semantics, logic, the scriptures
All this learning is of no use

To the beloved's country show me the way

What use are prayers and fasting, girl?
I have drunk from the pitcher of love

To the beloved's country show me the way

Bullah sits in the Lord's circle
He is free of rules and rituals

To the beloved's country show me the way

.16.

Fasts, Pilgrimages, Prayers

Fasts, prayers, pilgrimages, O Mother!
With the lover's coming, I forgot them all

When news of his arrival came
I forgot my grammar and logic

As his music began to play
fasts, prayers, pilgrimages gave way

Once the lover was in my home
I forgot what the holy books say

Everywhere you look, you can see him
Inside and outside he holds sway

People are deluded, O Mother!
Going after fasts, prayers, pilgrimages

Fasts, prayers, pilgrimages, O Mother!
With the lover's coming, I forgot them all

.17.

Toss the Prayers

Toss prayers in the fire, fasts in the mud, wipe out the holy verse
The husband is inside. Why then does the bride outside search?

.18.

Who Shall See God

Who shall see God, entirely on his love depends
God reveals himself to those who are his friends

.19.

Happiness

Judges are happy with bribes, death the mullahs pleases
Lovers are happy with music, their faith never decreases

.20.

The Hawkers Are Here

Mother, the hawkers are here
Hundreds of them
They call out to us
trading gems and diamonds

Hearing them call, I decide
I too will get myself diamonds
One to wear in each ear
and show everyone

I am completely ignorant
Can't tell a diamond from glass
No friends to help me bargain
No money do I have

When I ask them the price
I am left stunned
I who can't bear even a needle prick
is being asked for my head

Those who want these diamonds
must pay with their lives
Mother, the hawkers are here
Mother, the hawkers are calling

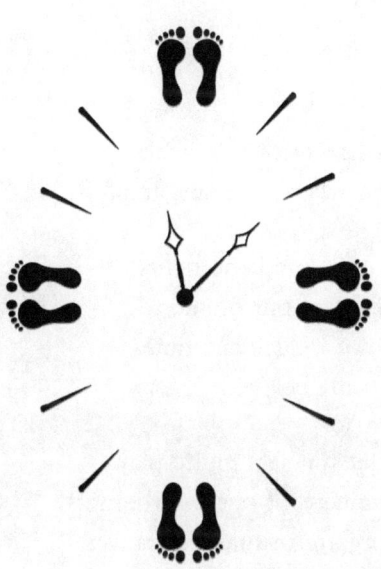

.21.

Sack the Timekeeper

Sack the keeper of the clock
The lover is coming home today

Let him not sound the hours
in this night of our reunion
Let him not reduce the time
I am with my beloved

Instead, let timeless music play
in this moment of our togetherness
I have forgotten ritual and prayer
drunk on the lover's presence

Oh! The beauty of seeing him
All my sorrows have vanished
Let this night go on forever
Oh! Build a wall against the dawn

.22.

Love Blossoms Ever New

Love blossoms ever new

Once I learnt love's lesson
I grew wary of the mosque
I found my way to the courtyard
where the music ever plays

Love blossoms ever new

When I discovered love's secrets
I was done with parrots and mynas
Purified from inside and out
Wherever I look I see the lover

Love blossoms ever new

Heer and Ranjha are already together
Yet Heer desperately calls for him
Remember yourself first, Heer,
in order to recognise him

Love blossoms ever new

Don't tire yourself reading the Vedas
or genuflecting five times in prayer
God is not in holy towns or in mosques
Those who have seen know him as light

Love blossoms ever new

Abandon the prayer rooms and mats
Throw away the beads and urns
Listen to the true lover's cry
God is beyond halal and haram

Love blossoms ever new

You wasted time in the mosque
Your insides unclean
Your prayers superficial
No point making a noise

Love blossoms ever new

When in love one forgets
even the ritual of prostration
Bullah sits quietly
Love takes him onwards

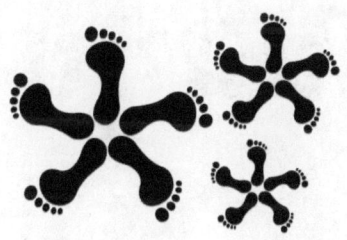

.23.

Calling to the Beloved

Calling for my beloved again and again
I have become him
Who should we call beloved now?
Union and separation no longer exist

Like Majnu in his mad devotion
turned into Laila
Calling for my beloved again and again
I have become him

Bulleh Shah, the lover is home
Why should I suffer taunts?
Calling the beloved again and again
I have become him

.24.

I Meditate on Your Name

I meditate on your name
I meditate on your name

The clay oven is useful
in its heat
You can cook food
for travelling fakirs
to come together and share

The pumice stone
is useful
in its roughness
Feet can be placed upon it
and scrubbed clean

Those who wish to find Him
must learn to surrender
like the lamb at the altar
is ready to be slaughtered
for God

I meditate on your name
I meditate on your name

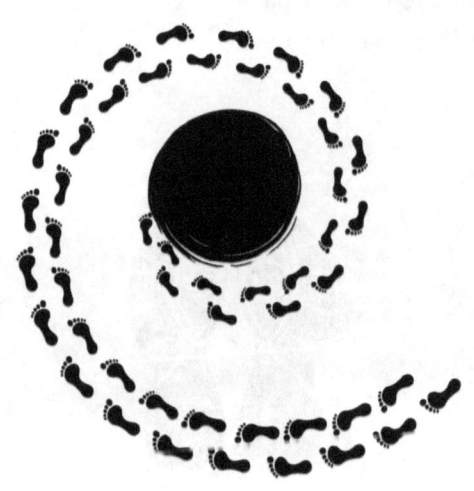

.25.

Ego

Cast your ego into the well, the A of Arrogance control
The lover will come home if you surrender body and soul

.26.

Who Will Recognise Me

Who will recognise me?
I am so different now

The teacher took my hand
and led me to the world that lies
beyond comings and goings
The beauty that lies past illusion

Who will recognise me?
I am so different now

He is beyond birth and death
and yet he came to me
as my lover
to lead me past duality

Who will recognise me?
I am so different now

He revealed to me his beauty
in various forms and guises
I have forgotten to be a crow
I walk with a swan's gait now

Who will recognise me?
I am so different now

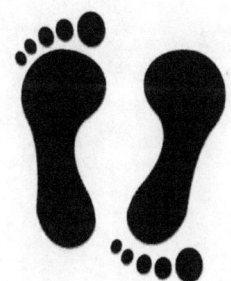

.27.

In the Grip of Love

He who is in the grip of love
dances with complete abandon

Knowing he has chosen his grief
people stare at him from afar
as he rips open his being
to discover himself within

The lover takes his orders
from the other realm
Knowingly he sips love's poison
Who can question that?

He who is in the grips of love
calls out for his lover repeatedly
He needs no music or accompaniment
to dance his soul's dance

Bullah found truth in love's city
and forgot everything else
He only speaks this truth today
so the true seeker may find beauty

He who is in the grip of love
dances with complete abandon

.28.

I Have Found Something

I have been given
a glimpse of the unfathomable

He is the enemy, He is the friend
He comes as Majnu, He is Laila as well
He is the teacher, He the pupil
He comes in many forms for us to know him

He lives in the mosque
He dwells in the temple
He wanders as a beggar
He sits on the sheikh's throne

He is the Turk on the prayer mat
He is the Hindu counting his beads
He is the veiled one, never to be seen
He is the one who visits you openly

Bullah is free of the ego
His work here is done
He has seen God inside himself
And in each and everyone

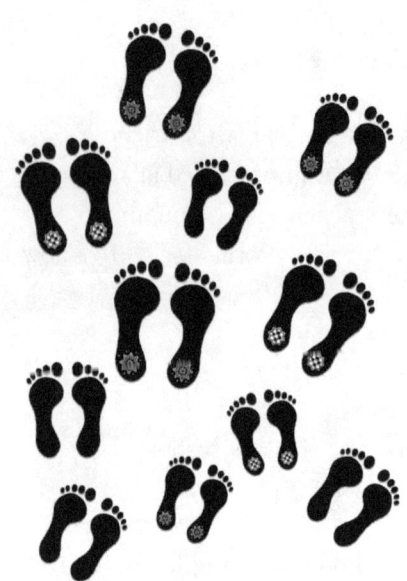

.29.

The Beloved Has Come as a Man

The beloved has come in the guise of a man

He is the deer, He the cheetah
He is the hunter too

The beloved has come in the guise of a man

He is the master, He the slave
He is the slave-trader too

The beloved has come in the guise of a man

He rides an elephant, He carries a begging bowl
He is the great yogi, He the wicked reveller

The beloved has come in the guise of a man

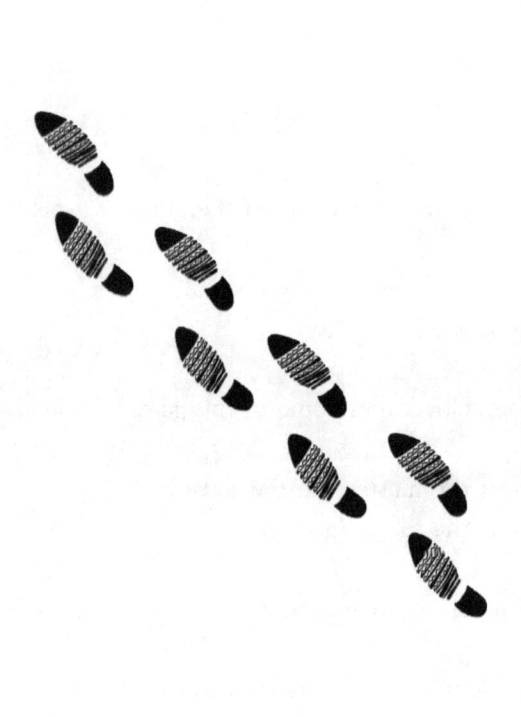

He is a master juggler, I a puppet
At his command I turn cartwheels

The beloved has come in the guise of a man

Cain and Abel were sons of Adam
Who was Adam born of, Bullah?

The beloved has come in the guise of a man

.30.
Clay

Bullah, I'm the potter's clay, it's not for me to say
Why I am this shape and not another way

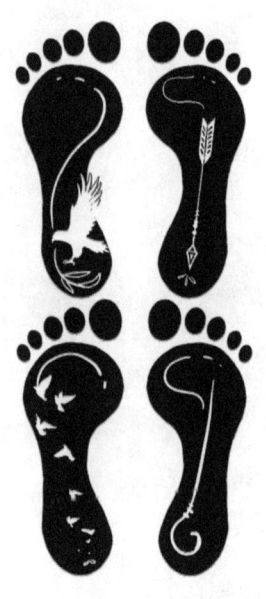

.31.

Fate

In the season of blossoms, birds came to peck
One was taken by the hawk, one caught in the hunter's snares
One dreamt of flying home, another was skewered
Bulleh Shah, it wasn't up to them, they simply lived their fate

.32.

Separation

Bullah, it's good to see the lover coming, not so to see him go
Brahmins and Sheikhs take to the forest, so intense is separation's woe

.33.

Let's Go to the Lover's Kitchen

Let's head to the lover's kitchen, Bullah, there's a butchering fest
Fat goats are being slaughtered, you might fail the test

.34.

The Lover Has Left

My lover has left
our neighbourhood
What now, God?

He wouldn't stay longer
Many followed him
What now, God?

Everywhere there is talk
of his leaving
What now, God?

Unable to see him
my heart is torn
What now, God?

Without his lover, Bulleh Shah
can neither swim nor drown
What now, God?

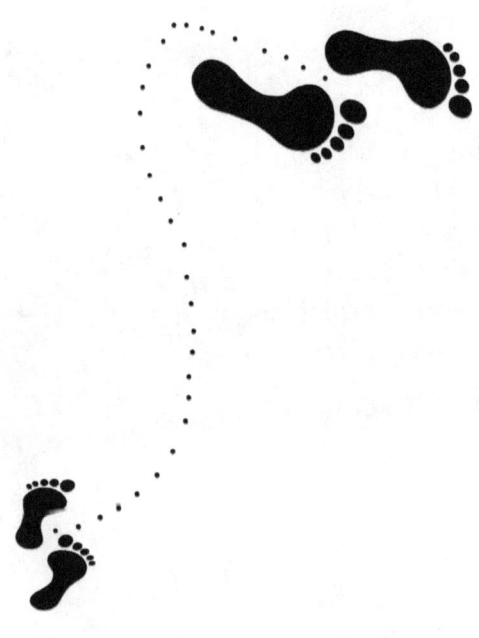

.35.

Turn Your Head Towards Us

Turn your heads towards us
Look this way, love

You have me on your hook
and you tug the line

One call from the heavens
and Mecca is astir

The Kheras put me in the palanquin
Resistance and pleading both fail

Mother, if you love the Kheras
find them another bride

Bullah is not ready to die yet
Let others die if they wish

Turn your heads towards us
Look this way, love

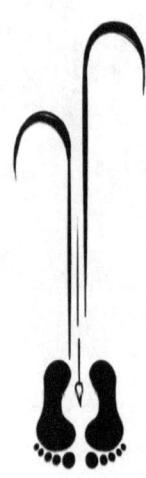

.36.

Let Me Merge

Let me merge in you
Make me one with you

You are the one
who awoke this love
Now hold my hand
and take me through

The path of love
is dangerous
I'm lost in the forest
Tigers and hyenas
surround me
and block my way

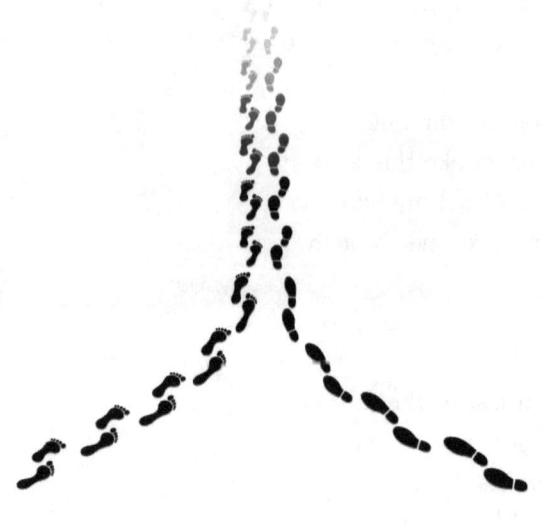

The tide is rising
My heart hammers
inside me
Take my boat
and guide me across

Don't forsake Bullah now
His worship is true
Be with me
till the veil is removed
and I have seen my bridegroom

Let me merge in you
Make me one with you

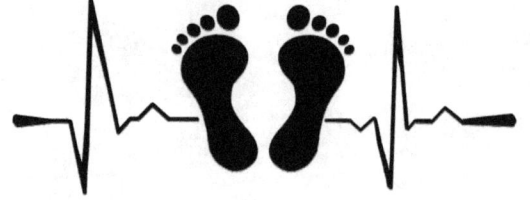

.37.

What's to Be Done

I am in love, what's to be done?
I cannot live or die without you

Listen to me, love
Day or night
I must have you
Without you
I weep
Without you
no sleep
I am in love
I am in pain
Need to see you again

I am in love, what's to be done?
Someone save Bullah from this plight

.38.

Waiting for Him

I'm sick at heart, chasing crows
I burn slowly as I wait for him

It's midnight, the stars are out
Some shine on, others drown
I walk towards the riverbank
Restless to cross to the other side

Not even a coin as fare
Yet I long to cross the river
I don't know the boatmen
We get into a quarrel

The riverbank is in confusion
And the river is in full spate
Even those who can swim go under
Who will pay heed to my foolish state?

I don't know my way across
I have no support, no oars even
My boat is battered and old
I can only weep and cry out loud

Across the Chenab, the forest is dense
and wild beasts roam through it
Tell me, what hope do I have then
of finding my lover and being with him?

Bulleh Shah, the lover must come home himself
wearing a crown and vermillion on his forehead
I will dress up to receive him
Seeing him I shall be well again

.39.

By the Riverbank

They come to fill their pots
And having filled them, leave
Some are coming, others going
Still others just stand there
with their arms stretched out

They come to fill their pots
And having filled them, leave

I am all dressed up
Necklace on my chest
Bangles on my arms
Hoops in my ears
But no signs of my man

They come to fill their pots
And having filled them, leave

Henna on my hands
Henna on my feet
Hair perfumed and combed out
Teeth clean and sparkling
But no signs of my man

They come to fill their pots
And having filled them, leave

Bulleh Shah, how do I find him?
What path shall I take?
I rolled the dice and lost
Deaf, mute, demented I stand
Alone by the riverbank

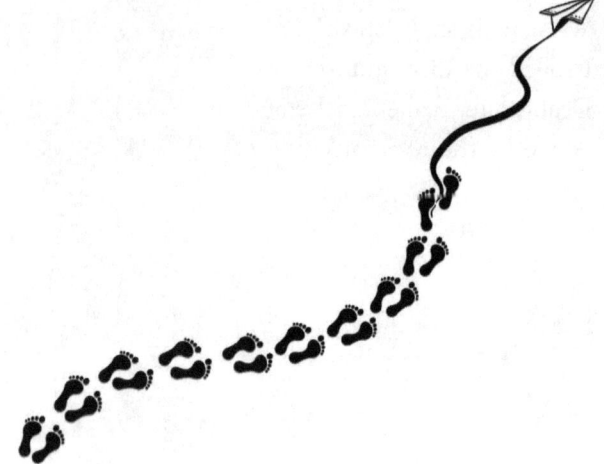

.40.

O Traveller

O traveller, bring me good news

I am wasted and bent
Convey my state to my lover
My hair is uncombed, in tangles
Don't hesitate to tell him
My message I will dictate
Convey it in strict confidence
Bulleh Shah longs for his lover

O traveller, go quickly, bring news

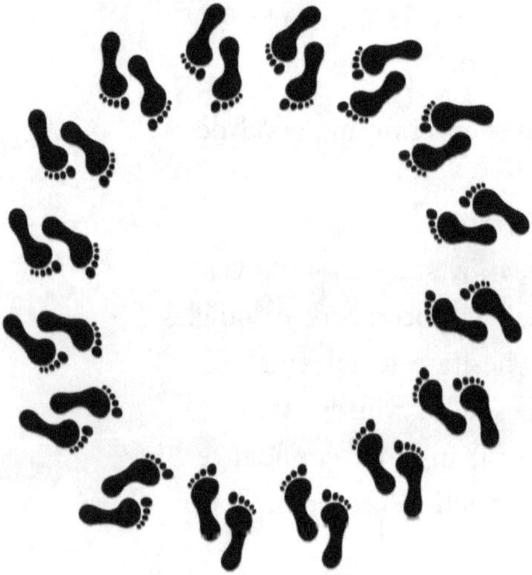

.41.

I'm in Love

I was love-struck from the beginning
From the very beginning of time

Love throws us into the fire
like seeds in a frying pan

Love asks us to die for it
when we have already died many times

Like an arrow stuck in the heart
the pain pierces through and through

Bullah, this love with the lord is odd
There is no merging with him

.42.

My Heart Is Yearning

Some talk and laugh
Others weep and wilt
Someone tell this blossoming spring
My heart is yearning for my lover

I'm standing bathed and dressed
The lover has left in anger
To hell with this finery
My heart is yearning for my lover

My enemies drive me crazy
I'm surrounded by grief on all sides
Come back home, let me see you
My heart is yearning for my lover

Bulleh Shah, the husband has come home
I hold my Ranjha in a tight embrace
My grief is banished across the seas
My heart is yearning for my lover

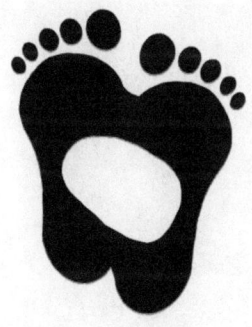

.43.

Heartless One

What a heartless man
I fell in love with
There is nothing to do
but cry now

What a heartless man
I fell in love with

Splintering the heart in two
he has gone and left
The body is bereft
The soul is gone with him

What a heartless man
I fell in love with

There is no trusting
one without a heart
The rustic laughs aloud
when a bird drops dead

What a heartless man
I fell in love with

He said he would return
but his promises are forgotten
I was such a fool
to love a heartless man

What a heartless man
I fell in love with

Bullah made a deal
Chose the poisoned cup
No profit, no loss
A basketful of woes

.44.

I Write to Shyam

I write to Shyam complaining
that I cannot see my lover
The courtyard looks scary
How do I spend the night alone?

I ask the pundits
To read their books and tell
Is there some fault in me?
Or is it my stars that are flawed?

Listen, soothsayers
Speak the truth
If I'm ill-fated
you must let me know

If I could run away I would
go become a wandering beggar
But held by the chains of love
I cannot move even a step

Sleep has become my enemy
It has moved to another country
If only I could sleep
I'd meet him in my dreams

Helplessly I used to weep
Each day more tearful than the last
But now my eyes are completely dry
As if someone has cast a spell

What has love given to me?
The hands are empty
The head wears a crown of thorns
And no way forward can I see

I pray to you my lover
Come take me away
To live in love's city
Don't try me any more

.45.

Don't Act Coy

Why do you hide behind the veil?
Why do you act all coy now?

Didn't you come yourself
and become manifest in everyone?
Did you not create this world
to engage with your own beauty?

I am drunk on your love
Don't ask me to behave respectably
Why should I not sing out loud
on this wine you poured for me?

You are the one who set this up
So don't act all coy now
I know you have come as Shah Inayat
Don't pretend to be shy now

Bullah is ready to be baked
in the fire of longing
Let the dross melt away
Only pure love remain

Why do you hide behind the veil?
Why do you act all coy now?

.46.

Stop It Now

Stop it now, enough of this
Sit with me, smile at me

You live in my heart
and yet act distant
Enough with showing off your powers
Now succumb to my magic
Enough of your cruelty
Enough of beating up one
who is already dying
for love of you
Enough of stifling me
This time I'll take aim
You be the target
Enough of running away
from me

Be still, I'll ensnare you
in my ribcage
I'm through with being
your slave girl
constantly beseeching you
Run, let's see
how far you can run
from me

Stop it now, enough of this
Sit with me, laugh with me

.47.

A Spell

I will weave such a spell
to bring my groom back

The heat of the sun
I will capture
with my magic spell
My eyes will be dark clouds
On my brows
will sit a storm
The seven seas will rage
inside my heart

I will flash like lightning
Become a cloudburst
Toss a few stars

into my love potion
and spread out the whiteness
of the moon to lie on
And sit down
and play a bewitching song

Such a spell I will cast
My bridegroom will come back
and I will be a woman
worthy of his love

.48.

In Love I Dance

I dance madly in the throes of love
In love's madness I dance away
Tiptap-tiptap-tiptap

You captured my heart
I drank from the poisoned cup willingly
Now the separation is killing me
Come back, oh, come back to me

I dance madly in the throes of love
In love's madness I dance away
Tiptap-tiptap-tiptap

I was a fool not to follow you
Now the sun is sinking low
Only the last rays of light remain
I will die if I don't see you again

I dance madly in the throes of love
In love's madness I dance away
Tiptap-tiptap-tiptap

Mother, don't try to stop me now
Who can call the boat back
after it has left the shore?
Oh, why did I let him go?

I dance madly in the throes of love
In love's madness I dance away
Tiptap-tiptap-tiptap

In the garden of my heart
A peacock dances for him
My lover is both Kiblah and Ka'aba
But wounding my heart he went away

I dance madly in the throes of love
In love's madness I dance away
Tiptap-tiptap-tiptap

Bulleh Shah, take me to Inayat's door
It is for him that I wear
this green and yellow skirt-blouse
It is for him that I dance

.49.

Come, Meet Me

Come and meet me, love
Ask how I am
For I'm surrounded
by sorrows

Separated from you
Lost in the wild
Preyed upon
by thugs and dacoits

The way shown by mullahs
only pits man against man
To do their bidding
is to walk into a trap

To follow the Shariat
is to wear shackles
What does the lover have
to do with caste and creed?

Across the river is love's country
Be careful of the greedy waves
But when the teacher holds the boat
then don't waste any time

Clamber onto the vessel
Have courage, have faith
The teacher is already there
Who looks for the sun
in the afternoon?

.50.

Ranjha Is All I Need

Give back my Ranjha to me
My Ranjha is all I need

He is my lover from before time
and this earth were manifest

Now he is off herding buffaloes
and I am left bereft

Give back to me my Ranjha
There is no one else for me

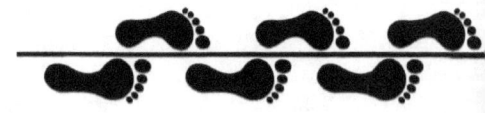

I stand draped in red
my eyes beautiful with longing

Between the lover and God
there is only a slight difference

Give back my Ranjha to me
My Ranjha is all I need

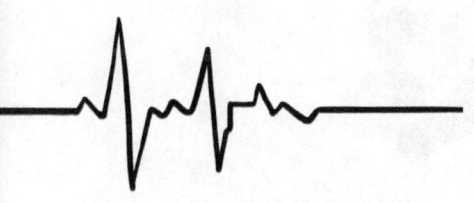

Ranjha! Ranjha! I Call

I have longed so long for Ranjha
That I have become him
Don't call me Heer
Henceforth Ranjha is my name

I am inside Ranjha
Ranjha lives in me
We are inseparable now
for I have become he
What we love we become
My caste is now the same as his

Drop the white robes, girl
White cloth betrays stains
Don ochre robes now
And dance to love's tune
Take me to Ranjha's village, Bulleya
Heer's home is no longer my place

.52.

Congratulate Me, Friends

Congratulate me, dear friends
I am married to my lover, Ranjha

It is such an auspicious day
My Ranjha has come to stay
Staff in hand, shawl on shoulders
He comes in a cowherd's garb

Congratulate me, dear friends

His crown is forgotten in the herd
His pedigree in the wilderness
But who fails to recognise God
Even if his identity is obscured?

Congratulate me, dear friends

Bulleh Shah has made his deal
Taken the poisoned cup to his lips
I have nothing to lose as
I chose this basket of woes

.53.

I Am Crazy

Let the hajis head for Mecca
My Ranjha is my Mecca
I am crazy like that

I belong to my Ranjha
Let my father throw me out
I am crazy like that

Let the hajis head for Mecca
My bridegroom is at home
I am crazy like that

I am my own haji, my own seeker
My heart houses thieves too
I am crazy like that

Let the hajis head for Mecca
I am off to Takht Hazara
I am crazy like that

The lover's home is Ka'aba
So say the holy books
I am crazy like that

.54.

Ranjha Has Come as a Jogi

Ranjha has come as a jogi
How he dazzles in that role

His eyes are deep-set
Like a tiger he watches me
Just looking at him
I forget my woes

I would know him anywhere
His ears are pierced
Around his neck are beads
He is as beautiful as Joseph

For this jogi I'll become a jogin
I will fetch water for him
My long-lost lover is here
The wasted years are forgotten

Bulleh Shah, this is my state
The lost lover is back again
How can I hide this?
Take me to Takht Hazara please

.55.

Why Should I Go to Ka'aba

Why should I go to Ka'aba
when my heart longs
for Takht Hazara?

Let others bow to Ka'aba
I bow to my lover

My heart longs for Takht Hazara

Seeing my flaws, Ranjha
Don't forsake me

My heart longs for Takht Hazara

Remember the promise you made
before time began

My heart longs for Takht Hazara

I cannot swim
Come and take me across

My heart longs for Takht Hazara

I have looked all over
There's no one else for me

My heart longs for Takht Hazara

Ranjha, take me, flaws and all
with you to the other side

My heart longs for Takht Hazara

Bulleh Shah's love is unique
Love him back unconditionally

Why should I go to Ka'aba
when my heart longs
for Takht Hazara?

.56.

The Good Days

Bullah, the good days are gone; at that time why didn't we pray
What is the use of repenting now? The birds have taken the crop away

.57.

Gathering Safflowers

The thorns have torn my scarf
The field's owner is cruel
I am tired of gathering safflowers

The guardians demand heavy taxes
Others gather less, my basket is full
I am tired of gathering safflowers

I'm barely done, the merchants arrive
Heavy the weight on my head, difficult my journey
I am tired of gathering safflowers

Those with good deeds go, leaving me behind
I whiled away my life, now I'm defeated
I am tired of gathering safflowers

I am mean, lowly, without any talents
I am undeserving of Shah Inayat's love
I am tired of gathering safflowers

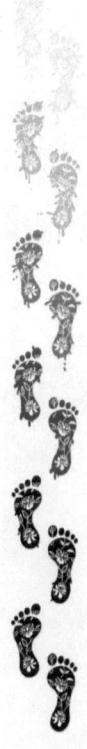

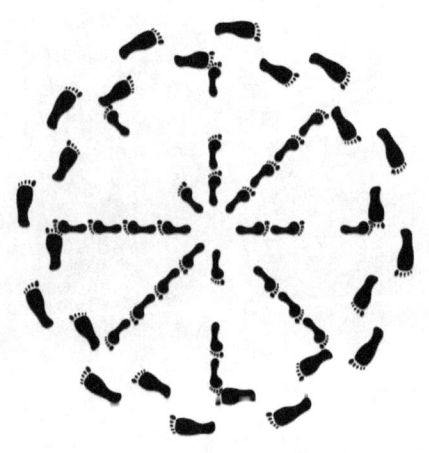

.58.

The Spinning Wheel Is Broken

The handle has come loose
The axle wobbles on its pin
Who'll fetch the ironsmith?
I can no longer spin

O blacksmith, fix the spindle
It sways, the thread breaks
No yarn does it make
I can no longer spin

No waxed thread, no connecting string
No grease on the straps
The driving band squeaks and groans
I can no longer spin

My friends call me to the spinning circle
But I'm too torn by grief to go
I have no sticks to roll the cotton in
I can no longer spin

My lover has taken the cows to graze
My heart has followed him to the glade
My eyes long to see him again
I can no longer spin

Who can take my message?
Beg him to come back to me
I'll spin hundreds of balls of cotton, Bullah
if my lord embraces me

.59.

Sisters, I Am Tired of Spinning

The threads lie forgotten in the back room
A lone cotton boll lies on my palm
The spinning wheel is in front,
the stool behind me
Sisters, I am tired of this spinning

What are jewels to me now?
Why should I gather a dowry?
What are these to one who is in love?
Catch the thief who stole my heart
Sisters, I am tired of this spinning

Spinning round and round again
The spindle breaks, the threads tangle
The beloved is like a butcher
The lover a goat for slaughter
Sisters, I am tired of this spinning

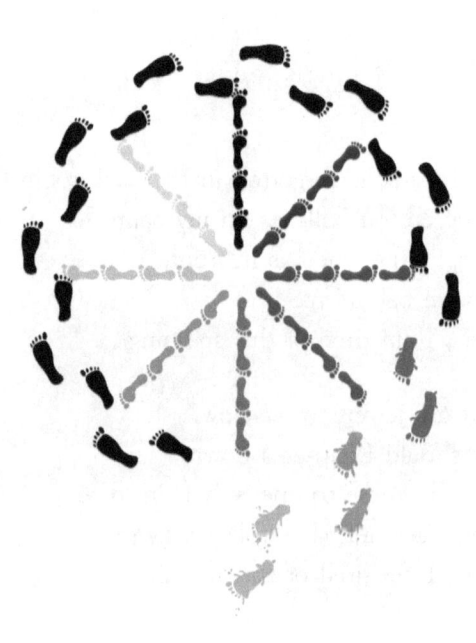

Let this spinning wheel break now
My soul be released from torment
Bullah, the lord leads us through
such a dance that the heavens roar
I cannot spin any more

.60.

Spin, Don't Be Idle

Spin, girl, don't be idle!

Pick the yarn, put it in the basket
Spin roll after roll
and you'll never need to wander naked

Spin, girl, don't be idle!

If you while away your days in idleness
the groom's arrival will catch you unprepared
Who will save you then, girl?

Spin, girl, don't be idle!

Your parents have fixed your wedding day
Time is scarce, don't throw it away
No turning back, in the in-laws' place you'll stay

Spin, girl, don't be idle!

Without a dowry no one will want you
How will you please the husband, pray?
Girl, pay heed to what the fakirs say

Spin, girl, don't be idle!

Your companions' wedding dresses are ready
Girl, why were you led astray?
When you get there you'll understand the truth

Spin, girl, don't be idle!

Bullah, the husband cares not for bangles and anklets
Only if you have virtue will he embrace you
Else you'll weep tears of blood, girl

Spin, girl, don't be idle!

.61.

Gold

Bullah, let's go to the jewellers where many ornaments are sold
They may appear different, but all are made of gold

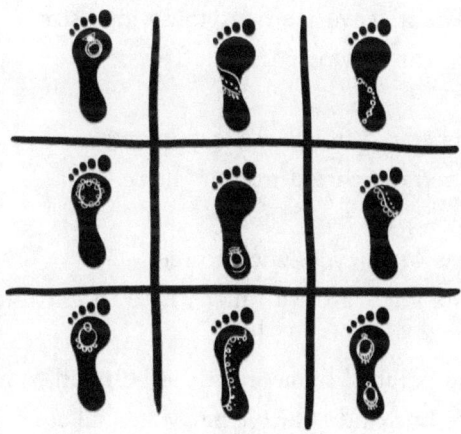

Gather Around Me, Precious Girlfriends

Gather around me, precious girlfriends
To the in-laws' place I have to go
God knows, your day will come too

My parents gave me one blouse, one scarf
Seeing this dowry, copiously I wept

I'm separated from my companions
Like a crane parted from its flock

Thorns of all types stick to me
Today's griefs are with me; where to put tomorrow's?

In the parents' home even the best can't stay
To the husband's place, one by one, all are called away

He embraces only those who come with virtues
Gather around me, precious girlfriends
To the in-laws' place I have to go

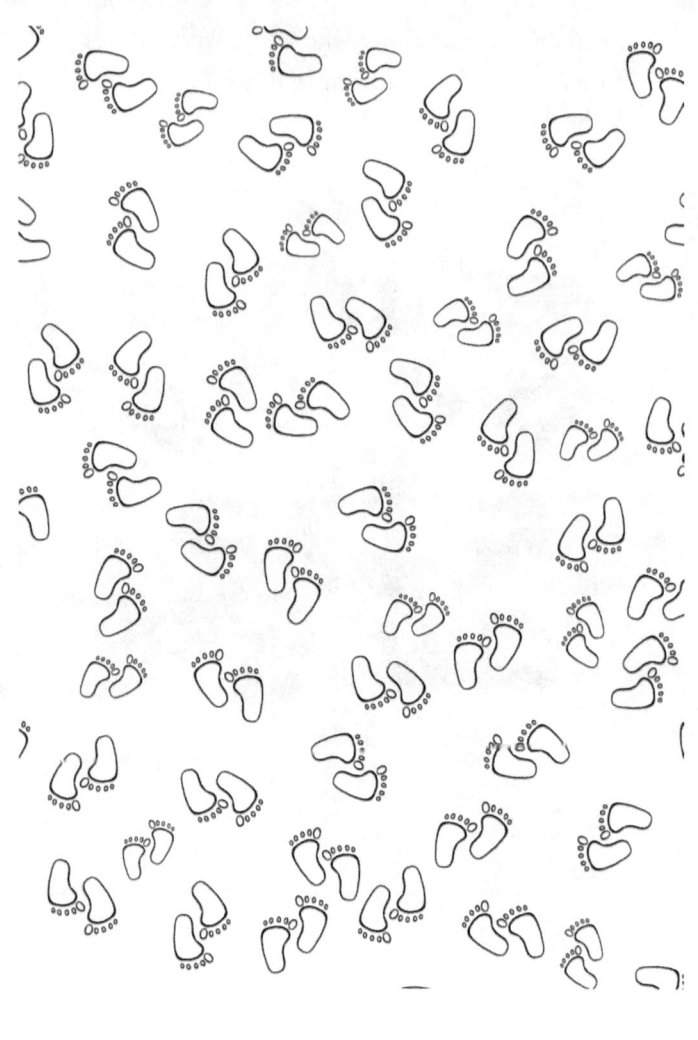

.63.

Cotton

Warp, woof, bobbins, shuttles, spools
Each has a different name
Each demands a separate place
Yet, bolls of cotton are all the same

Muslin, poplin, cambric, flannel
Are all different fabrics
And garments come with different names
Yet the cotton they are made of is the same

Girls show off their different rings bearing different names
Their ornaments can be different bangles or bracelets
But the silver they are fashioned out of is the same
Cotton has only one colour

He may graze goats or sheep
Look after buffaloes or pigs
Or take cows out to pasture
The herdsman is the same

Bullah, why ask the Lord's caste
Give thanks for his mercy instead
If you desire the joys of spring
Remain a servant of the Master

.64.

Khaki

Of dust we're made
To dust we'll return

Those who leave
never come back
Beloveds, friends, lovers
who couldn't live without us
However much you cry
their graves do not answer
Such is death's way

No resting
this way or that
We sit among the living
feeling worse than death
Today or tomorrow
It will be here
There's no escaping death's ire

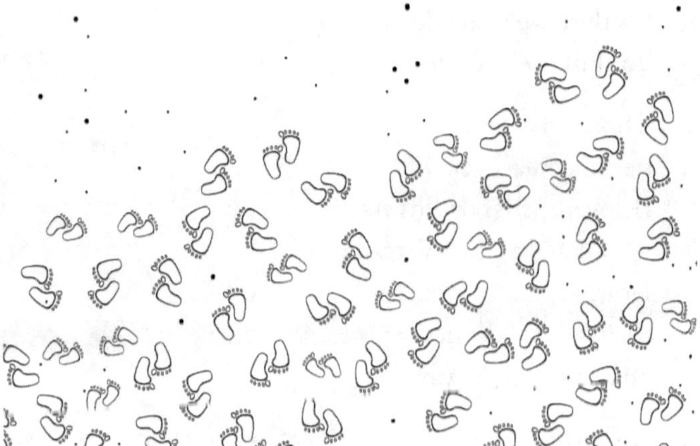

Chased by death's pawns
we have reached this far
Here too we cannot stay
Where should we go?
We too must follow
the others gone before
into death's fold

Bullah, no one gets to stay
Crying, protesting, all must go
Only God's name is currency
Nothing else can we hold
I am an illusion
This world is illusory
Everyone, everything, a dream

Of dust we're made
To dust we'll return

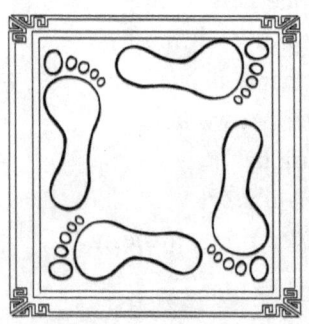

.65.

Live Quietly

Live quietly and get by

No one likes the truth
They pounce on you
Avoid sitting next to you
if you speak the truth

Live quietly and get by

Only to the lover
truth comes like a bridegroom
and removes the veil
Truth brings new growth

Live quietly and get by

The lover cannot escape
from the perfume of truth
in the bridal chamber
The world becomes useless

Live quietly and get by

Bulleh Shah reveals this reality
Truth is above the Shariat
Truth is the way
to the state of union

.66.

Make the Ganga Flow Backwards

O seeker, make the Ganga flow backwards
Then you'll get a glimpse of God

Cotton balls of love on your palm, the axle steady in hand
Spindle of knowledge, the spinning wheel of meditation
Now spin it backwards
Let Kumbhkaran go back the route he came
Let the secret of Lanka become unrevealed
Let Ravan, the ten-headed one, stand undestroyed
Take Lakshman back to when the unstruck music played
Leave the guru's feet, leave being his servant

Go back to when you were one with Him
when everything all around was God

Enter the realm of pure bliss, O Seeker
Make the Ganga flow backwards

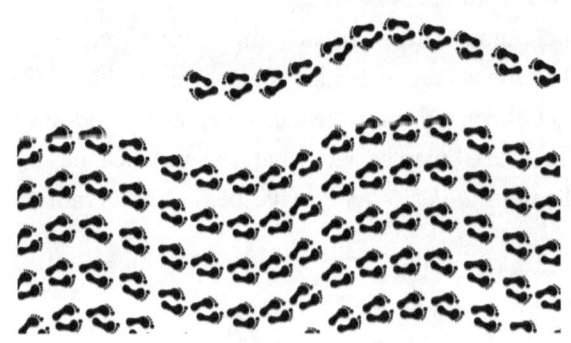

.67.

Sweeper

I am a sweeper
at the service
of the true lord

Meditation is my duster
Knowledge my broom
Anger and lust I sweep

I am a sweeper
at the service
of the true lord

I ask no favours
of the priest or doctor
Only to stay and serve

I am a sweeper
at the service
of the true lord

Night and day
This is what I ask
To serve Inayat Shah

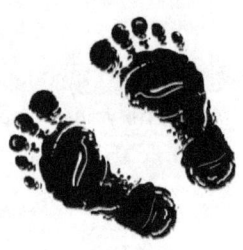

.68.
Keep Away

Traders dwell in holy shelters, in temples thugs stay
Charlatans fill mosques, lovers just keep away

.69.

The Only Place

Don't look in holy places, nor where the pious give out food
Not in the crowded mosque, encountering the mullah's grim face
Outside rich men's houses you'll find guards are stood
To find solace for the heart's woes, God's door is the only place

.70.

With This Knowledge I'm Ablaze

With this knowledge I'm ablaze

We don't have to be Hindu or Turk
To be accepted follow love's way
It is the lover who wins God over

With this knowledge I'm ablaze

The thugs just make a noise
Mislead with talk of birth and death
Only the lover can experience God

With this knowledge I'm ablaze

Bullah, the ways of love are different
No useless noise, love is steadfast
In silence it hears God's voice.

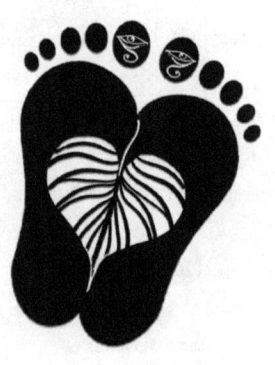

.71.

Finding God

If God was to be found
by washing and bathing
frogs and fishes would find him

If God was to be found
by roaming in the wilderness
cows and calves would have him

Listen to Bulleh Shah
God comes to the pure of heart
those truthful in their ways

.72.

Eat What Is Forbidden

Bullah, eat what is forbidden, be in gratitude
Leave the mosque, avoid torment, seek solitude
Don't ask riddles whose answers are hidden
Come, let's go, where wine is not forbidden

.73.

Drink Wine

Bullah, drink wine, eat kebabs, use your bones as fuel
Go burgle God's house, go rob that thug most cruel

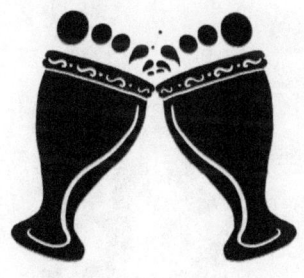

.74.

Say Yes

Bullah, as a lover of God, learn to play small
When they call you an infidel, say yes-yes to all

.75.

People Tell Bullah

People tell Bullah, *Go sit in the mosque all day*
Useless the mosque if with the heart you don't pray
No use your ablutions if the insides are not clean, I say
Prayers are a waste, a Master's grace shows the way

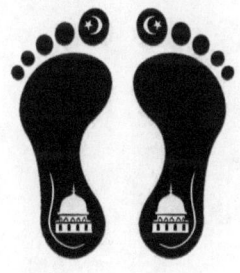

.76.

If God Came to the Temple

Bullah, if God came to the temple, he would say
Bring in the fools, send the pundit away

.77.

The Thief

The thief is tucked in my folds
Hey, the thief is right inside
Whom should I call out to?
Oh, whom should I tell?
The thief has run out into the world
The thief is causing an uproar
The thief is raising hell

The Muslims are scared of the pyre
The Hindus avoid the grave
Both are dying of the fear
of each other's way
One is called Ramdass
The other Fateh Mohammed
For ages this has caused furore
If only they'd understand
the same thief sits inside them
and give up the uproar

Those who are smart
have recognised him
and put all their quarrels to rest
But others are like peacocks
strutting about in vain
thinking themselves masters
while the thief who owns us all
is laughing at the jest

The call of the first muezzin
of Baghdad
can be heard today in Lahore
You may think you see me
dancing here
But it is Shah Inayat
who pulls the strings
Arrest Bulleh Shah's thief
And bring him forth

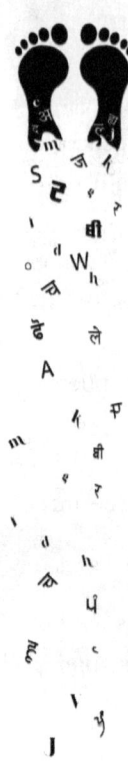

.78.

Be Done with Learning

Be done with learning, friend
All you need is one alphabet

There is no end to learning
But life will pass you by
All you need is one alphabet
So be done with learning, friend

Enough of reading and writing
Enough of your holy books
They seem to cast light
But there is darkness within

You meditate, you prostrate
You call out from minarets
And lecture from the stage
Yet you lack true faith

What good is this learning?
You call the seeing man blind
You create hurdles for the good
And encourage the thieves

Your learning gives you stature
but creates problems in its wake
The ignorant are cheated
and misled with false words

And though you might become a scholar
Remember God loves the simple man
Your learning unleashes desires
These desires become your undoing

You make your living off debates
These are the wages of sin
You say something, do something else
Your own life is a falsehood

When I learnt the lesson of love
I plunged headlong into duality
I was lost and would have drowned
But Shah Inayat took me across

.79.

A Simple Truth Ends the Matter

A simple truth ends the matter

Forget your calculations
Stay away from doubt
Dismiss thoughts of hell and heaven
Banish imaginary concerns
Truth enters a clear mind

A simple truth ends the matter

No use that forehead to the ground
No point prostrations in the mosque
You read the Kalma to show off
with no understanding in your heart
Can the truth remain hidden?

A simple truth ends the matter

Many return as hajjis
wearing robes of blue
They profit from going on Haj
Is this how it should be?
Can the truth remain hidden?

A simple truth ends the matter

Some go to the forest
live on a single grain
needlessly exhausting the body
coming home again wasted
All this to no avail

A simple truth ends the matter

Find a master, love creation
Sink into mystic abandon
No desires, no bonds
Let your heart be clean
Bullah, the truth cannot remain hidden

A simple truth ends the matter

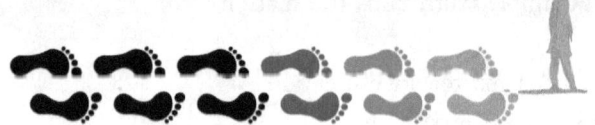

.80.

The Matter Doesn't End

It doesn't end by going to Mecca
and prostrating a hundred times

It doesn't end by going to the Ganga
and taking a hundred holy dips

It doesn't end by going to Gaya
and chanting a hundred chants

Bulleh Shah, the matter doesn't end
till you remove the I from inside your self

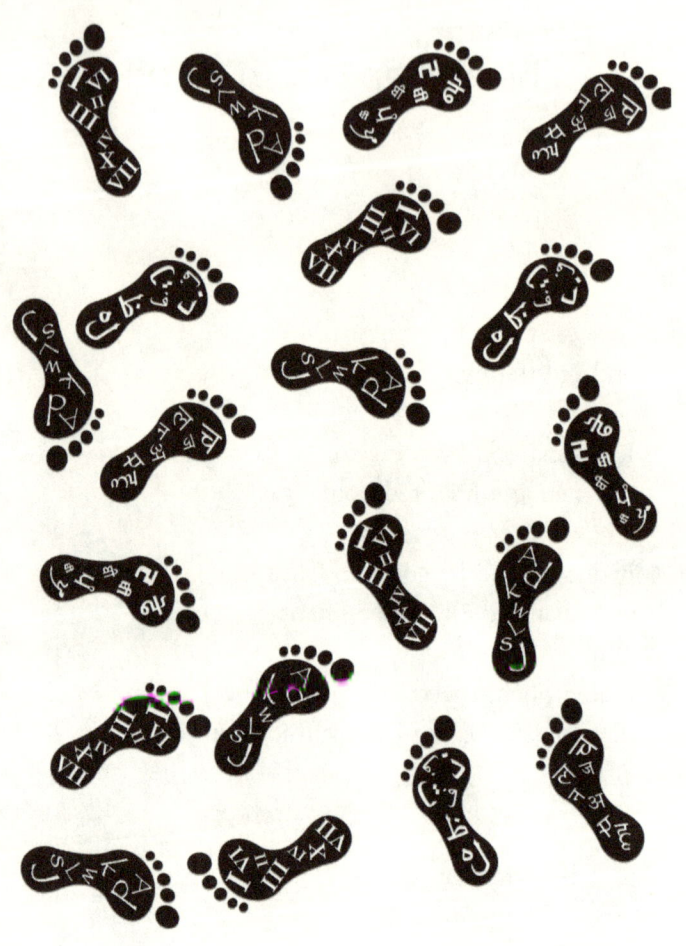

.81.

Go Beyond Reading

You read so many books
You became a learned scholar
You never cared to read your self

You visited mosques and temples
but left unexplored
your own heart's realms

You battled everyday with the devil
Did you never think
to fight your own ego first?

Bulleh Shah, you chased distant goals
and forgot the one who dwells within

.82.

From the Half-Learned I Flee

I flee from the half-learned
I flee from the half-learned

If the discerning question me
I confess this willingly

From the half-learned I flee
From the half-learned I flee

The learned are my brothers
The half-knowers drive me crazy

I'd rather swing with love
Save me from the half-learned

.83.

Hats Off 1

Bullah, hats off to those who beguile with words and lead astray
They'll gift you a nail, but keep the anvil hidden away

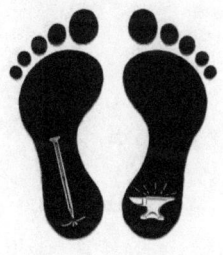

.84.

Hats Off 2

Bullah, hats off to those who talk big and appeal
Lost pennies they return, the purse they conceal

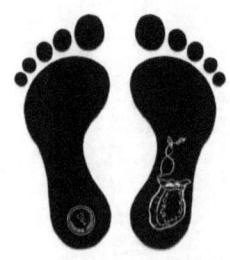

.85.

Don't Pray for Forgiveness

Don't pray for forgiveness
What kind of repentance is that?

Your lips pray, your heart is untouched
You cling to your vices
even as you beg forgiveness
Why should you be forgiven?

Don't pray for forgiveness
What kind of repentance is that?

You do what is forbidden
Steal from your fellow man
Take false oaths upon the holy book
And expect that you should be trusted?

Don't pray for forgiveness
What kind of repentance is that?

You give money to the poor
looking to multiply it
How can you live off usury
and call yourself a Muslim?

Don't ask for forgiveness
It means nothing at all

You may live a hundred days
but one day you will die
You'll regret this false repentance
and be afraid of God

Don't ask for forgiveness
It means nothing at all

Those who unleash suffering
and are not scared of God
will suffer for their sins
in this world and beyond

Don't ask for forgiveness
It means nothing at all

Listen to Bulleh Shah's truth
He has found true guidance
Shah Inayat is his guide
and will take him across

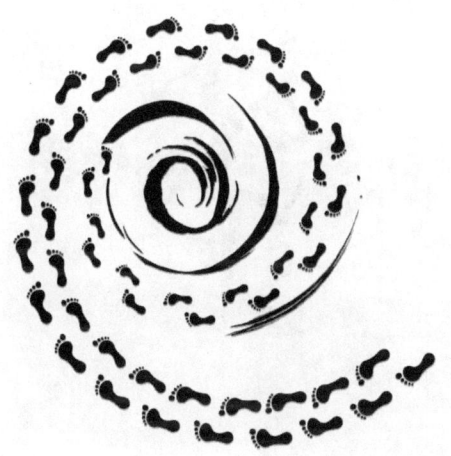

.86.

Where Do You Come From

Where have you come from?
Where are you headed to?
Tell me your destination

The position you're so proud of
Know that it will not go with you

You who have tortured, oppressed and stolen
from people their food and livelihood

Your four days of ruling will get over
and it will be time for you to go

Death is a relentless boatman
He will row you across to the other shore

He will take you to the silent city
in the country where all must go

Where have you come from?
Where are you headed to?
Tell me your destination

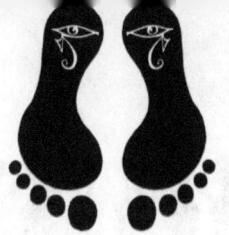

.87.

Your God Is Distant

You see light in the Ka'aba miles away
But can't see God in my infidel soul, you say
Your God is so far, mine lives near
Your intentions are suspect, I fear

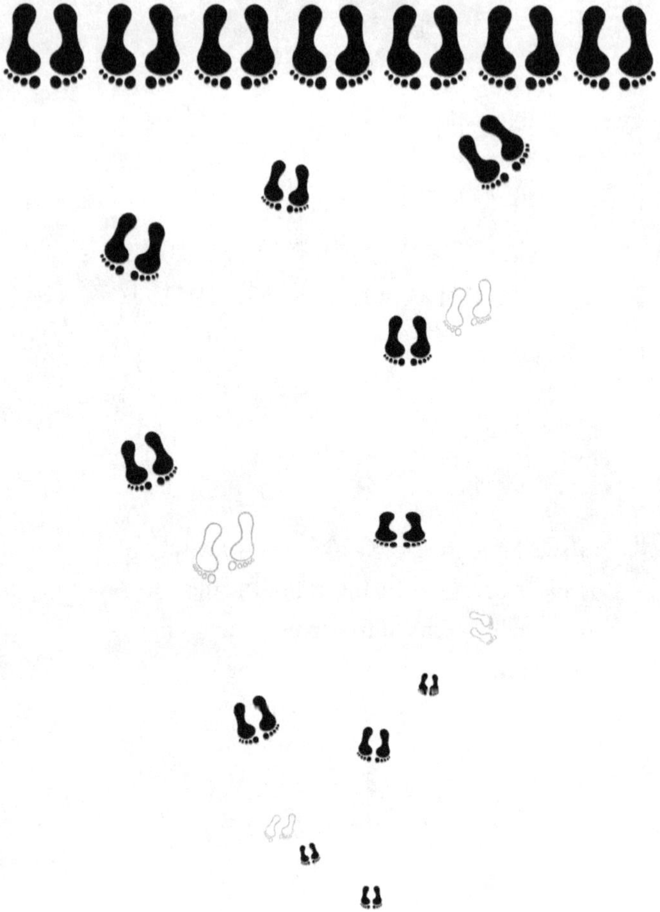

.88.

The Times Are Perverse

The times are perverse
so we may find Him
Sparrows prey on falcons
Crows kill eagles
Horses are fed rubbish
while donkeys graze on grass

Love has left us completely
No loving uncles, no respected elders
Even fathers abhor their sons
while daughters are cold to mothers

Truth is given short shrift
and falsehood decorated
Achievers have become paupers
while backbenchers are celebrated

Those with coarse shawls rule
while the kings are out begging
Bullah it is as God decrees
Who can argue with it?

The times are perverse
dragging us closer to Him

.89.

The Play of Clay

Look how the clay is acting up
The clay is at play, friend!

Clay horse, clay armour
The horseman too is clay
Clay chases clay
Clay slays clay
with weapons of clay
Clay seeks to conquer clay
Clay proudly owns more clay
and puts it on display
Gardens of clay
sprout flowers of clay
Clay stands applauding
the wonders of clay
Creatures of clay

laugh for a bit
and then lie down
six feet under it

Shrug off your burdens, Bullah
Understand the play of clay
The clay is at play, friend!

.90.

Dogs Do Better

You're up till late
in prayer
Dogs bark all night
Dogs do better

You suffer
for your faith
Dogs sleep on garbage
Dogs do better

You are very devoted
However, after being kicked
dogs return to their Master
Dogs do better

Bulleh Shah says
Add a spark
to your worship
lest the dogs do better

.91.

Unless We Experience Love

Unless we experience love
we're like needles without thread
Love is the great giver
Through love we know ecstasy

Those who feel love in their bones
have experienced death while living
Love is our father and mother
Through love we know ecstasy

Standing alone under a tree
A lover's body wastes away
When two lovers are together
wickedly they laugh with glee

Whoever falls in love
becomes helpless in it
Love pervades his every cell
He cannot conceal it

Wherever he looks he sees God
Bullah, a lover is always saved
Anxious to find his beloved's home
He meets and talks to God

God peeps from inside the heart
Through love we know ecstasy

.92.

Wake Up, Traveller

Wake up now, traveller
The stars are gone
It is time for dawn

As you sleep at the inn
with your fellow travellers
can you not hear the conch
blowing to herald the morn?

Get your work here done
For you will not return
Can't you hear the call
to wake up and come?

Let go those gems, those diamonds
They will be of no use there
Though the sea is very large
it cannot sate a man's thirst

Only your good deeds count
So tend your fields with care
Don't let the deer of desire
wreak its havoc there

Wake up now, traveller
The stars are gone
It is time for dawn

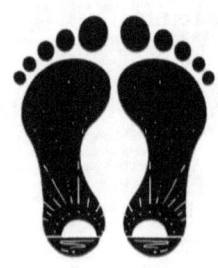

.93.

That Friend

Bullah, who is that supreme friend of yours of whom it is said
He holds the Quran in his hand, wears on his neck the holy thread?

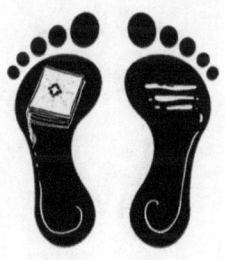

.94.

God Is Light

God is light, the world illusion
Behind the veil, his face is hidden

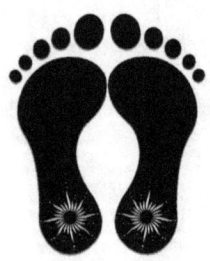

.95.

Play in the Courtyard

Play in this courtyard with abandon

It has a nice alcove
In the alcove, a window
Place your bed there
for a night with the beloved

The courtyard has nine doors
The tenth door is shut
Not knowing where he'll enter from
The entire street is a mystery

Play in this courtyard with abandon

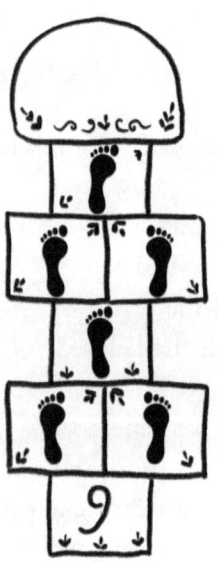

It has a nice alcove
In the alcove, a window
At every turn of the spinning wheel
remember the beloved

In this courtyard, a spirited elephant
strains at its chains
Bulleh Shah, servant of the lord,
wakens those who are awake

Play in this courtyard with abandon

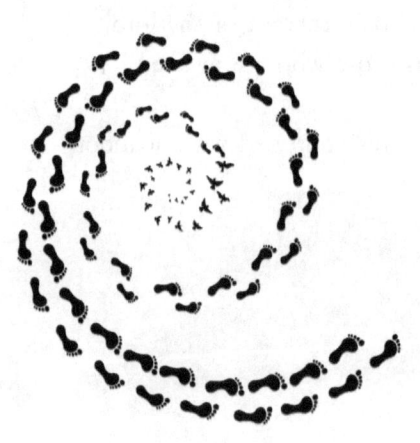

.96.

Let's Go and See

Let us go and see the wild one
The one they talk of in the spinning circle
The one who cares not for our caste
The one who draws us into the ocean of unity

About him there is a clamour everywhere
He remains beside us always
He is nearer, he tells us
He is within us, he says

Leave this world of falsity
Remain intoxicated with love
Those who find the lover
are deaf, blind and dumb

He's not yours, he's not mine
This world's quarrels are false
Without a master there's no escape
Remember him, he'll remember you

Bullah shares a hint
with those seeking him
Recall the sign in the trader's house
God's hands cover his followers'

Let us go and see the wild one
The one they talk of in the spinning circle

River of Unity

What to say about him?
Look how he behaves

We are his family
Yet, there is this veil

Sometimes he reads the namaz
At other times he worships idols

Although there is only one of him
he lives in a million homes

Everywhere you look, he's there
He is everyone's friend

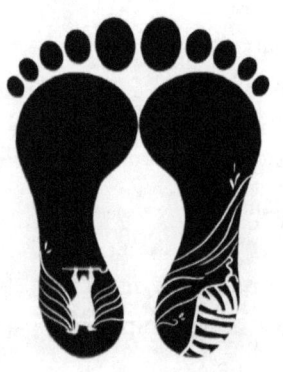

He made both Moses and Pharoah
Yet with each other they fight

Why are some sent to hell
when He himself made all?

We are people of one country
Why are some buried, some burnt?

Look beyond this world's duality
There is a river there
where everyone swims
He is here, there, everywhere
The servant, the master
Bullah, such is his game
He does everything
He does nothing

.98.

Let's Go to the Fair

Come, let's head to the fair, fakirs
There where the unstruck music plays
Limitless, with no end or beginning
Listening to this music
shed all falsehood, all illusion
This music befriends all
The pipe is impartial

Come, let's head to the fair, fakirs
If it doesn't bring you into union
you have gained nothing
neither capital nor interest
The way of the fakir is difficult
Hold steady your mind, lover
Man and Master are one
Bullah, let go of the world

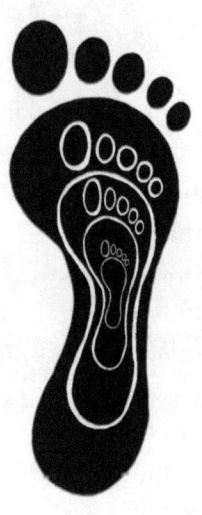

.99.

You

You created this palace of elements, and you sit inside
You are the girls, you the boys, you their parents
You it is who lives and dies, and you the mourner
Bullah, God created the world and it's his to take care of

.100.

Who

If you are outside, then who do I feel inside?
If you are inside, don't you feel confined?
You are everywhere, you are in everyone
You are in me, you are in you, you are everything
Who is this we call Bullah then?

Index of Punjabi Poems

Aa Mil Yaar Saar Lai Meri — Come Meet Me, 49
Aao Faqiro Mele Chaliye — Let's Go to the Fair, 97
Aao Saiyo Ral Dio Ni Vadhai — Congratulate Me, Friends, 52
Ab Hum Gum Huye Prem Nagar Ke Shahar — I Am Lost, 5

Ab Lagan Lagi Ki Kariye — What's to Be Done, 37
Aisa Jagiya Gian Palita — With This Knowledge, 70
Apne Sang Ralain Piare — Let Me Merge, 36
Bas Kar Ji Hun Bas Kar Ji — Stop It Now, 46
Bhaina Main Katdi Katdi Hutti — Sisters, I Am Tired, 59
Bullha Ki Jana Main Kaun — Bullah, How Do I Know, 2
Bullhe Nu Samjhavan Aayian Bhaina Te Bharjayian — They Come to Reason, 11

Chalo Dekhiye Us Mastanre Nu — Let's Go and See, 96

Chup Karke Karin Guzare Nu — Live Quietly, 65
Dhola/Maula Aadmi Ban Aya — The Beloved Has Come, 29
Dil Loche Mahi Yaar Nu — My Heart Is Yearning, 42
Ghariyali Dio Nikal Ni — Sack the Timekeeper, 21
Hathi Dhilak Gayi Mere Charkhe Di — The Spinning Wheel Is Broken, 58

Hindu Na Nahin Musalman	Neither Hindu nor Muslim, 3
Hun Mainu Kaun Pehchane	Who Will Recognise Me, 26
Ik Alif Parho Chhutkara He	A Is for Allah, 4
Ik Nukte Vich Gal Mukdi He	A Simple Truth Ends the Matter, 79
Ik Ranjha Mainu Lorida	Ranjha Is All I Need, 50
Ilmon Bas Kareen O Yaar	Be Done with Learning, 78
Ishq Di Navion Naveen Bahar	Love Blossoms Ever New, 22
Ishq Haqiqi Ne Muthi Kure	To the Beloved's Country, 15
Je Rabb Milda	Finding God, 71
Jichar Na Ishq Majazi Lage	Unless We Experience Love, 91
Jis Tan Lagya Ishq Kamal	In the Grip of Love, 27
Katt Kure Na Vat Kure	Spin, Don't Be Idle, 60
Khaki Khak Syun Ral Jana	Khaki, 64
Khed Lai Vich Vehre Ghumi Ghum	Play in the Courtyard, 95
Ki Bedardan Sang Yaari	Heartless One, 43
Ki Kardan Ni Koi Puchho	River of Unity, 98
Kyun Ohle Bah Bah Jhaki Da	Don't Act Coy, 45
Maati Kudam Karendi Yaar	The Play of Clay, 89
Main Bekaid Main Bekaid	I Am Free, 6
Main Choohretri Han Sachhe Sahib Di Sarkaron	Sweeper, 67
Main Kusumbra Chun Chun Hari	Gathering Safflowers, 57

Main Kyun Kar Jawan Kabe Nu	Why Should I Go to Ka'aba, 55
Main Pa Parhian Ton Nasna Han	From the Half-Learned I Flee, 82
Main Paya He Main Paya He	I Have Found Something, 28
Mainu Ishq Hulare Denda	On Love's Swings, 14
Mainu Ki Hoya Hun Maithon Gayi Gawati Main	What Happened to Me, 7
Makkeh Gaya Gal Mukdi Nahi	The Matter Doesn't End, 80
Meri Bukkal De Vich Chor	The Thief, 77
Mil Layo Sahelrio Meri Raj Gahelrio	Gather Around Me, 61
Murli Baaj Uthi Anghatan	The Sound of the Flute, 8
Ni Main Kamli Haan	I Am Crazy, 53
Ni Mainu Lagra Ishq Awal Da	I'm in Love, 41
Nit Parhna En Istighfar	Don't Pray for Forgiveness, 84
Paandhiyan Ho	O Traveller, 40
Padh Padh Ilm Hazaar Kitaban	Go Beyond Reading, 81
Pani Bhar Bhar Gayian Sabhe	By the Riverbank, 39
Pattian Likhungi Main Sham Nu	I Write to Shyam, 44
Piaria Sanoon Mithra Na Lagda Shor	The Noise No Longer Pleases, 13
Piya Piya Karte Hamin Piya Huye	Calling to the Beloved, 23
Raatin Jagen Karen Ibadat	Dogs Do Better, 90

Rain Gayi Latke Sabh Tare	Wake Up, Traveller, 92
Ranjha Jogira Ban Aya	Ranjha Has Come as a Jogi, 54
Ranjha Ranjha Kardi Ni Main Aape Ranjha Hoi	Ranjha Ranjha I Call, 51
Roze Haj Namaz Ni Maye	Fasts, Pilgrimages, Prayers, 16
Sabh Iko Rang Kapahin Da	Cotton, 63
Sade Wal Mukhra Mor Ve Piariya	Turn Your Head, 35
Se Vanjare Aye Ni Maye	The Hawkers Are Here, 20
Tangh Mahi Di Jalian	Waiting for Him, 38
Tera Naam Tehieda	I Meditate on Your Name, 24
Tere Ishq Nachaya Kar Thaiya Thaiya	In Love I Dance, 48
Toone Kaman Karke Ni Main Piyara Yaar Manavangi	A Spell, 47
Toon Kidhron Aya Kidhar Jana	Where Do You Come From, 86
Toon Nahinon Main Nahin Ve Sajna	Only You, 12
Ulte Hor Zamane Aye	The Times Are Perverse, 88
Ulti Ganga Bahayo Re Sadho	Make the Ganga Flow Backwards, 66
Uth Gaye Gawandhon Yaar	The Lover Has Left, 34
Vekho Ni Ki Kar Gaya Mahi	Look What He's Done, 10
Wah Wah Ramaz Sajan Di Hor	The Lover's Style, 9

Bibliography

Books

Duggal, K.S. *The Mystic Muse: Sain Bulleh Shah*. New Delhi: Abhinav Publications, 1996.

Gibbons, Bob, and Pritchard-Jones, Siân. 'Introduction'. In *Bulleh Shah: A Sufi Mystic of the Punjab*. Pilgrims Pocket Books. Varanasi: Pilgrims Publishing, 2008.

Gill, Harjeet Singh. *Sufi Rhythms*. Patiala: Publication Bureau, Punjabi University, 2007.

Krishna L.R. *Punjabi Sufi Poets (AD 1460–1900)*. Bombay: Oxford University Press, 1938.

Rafat, Taufiq. *Bulleh Shah: A Selection*. New Delhi: Vanguard Publications, 1982.

Shackle, Christopher. *Bulleh Shah's Sufi Lyrics: Selections from a World Classic*. Murty Classical Library of India, 2015.

Singh, Harbhajan, and Nadvi, Shaib. *Bulleh Shah*. New Delhi: Hind Pocket Books, 2006.

Syed, Najm Hosain. *Recurrent Patterns in Punjabi Poetry*. Lahore: Justin Group, 2006.

Research Papers & Articles

Hussain, Ashna. *Politics, Poetry and Pluralism: Bulleh Shah in the Late Mughal Empire*. Thesis, Western Sydney University, 2018.

Puri, Rakshat. *Bulleh Shah in Punjabi Poetic Tradition*. Apna.org

Sadiq, Atia. *Kafi: A Genre of Sufi Punjabi Poetry*. Lahore: University of Punjab, 2013.

Soofi, Mushtaq. 'Punjab Notes: Punjabi Language and Historical Records'. *Dawn*, 6 March 2023.

Websites

https://www.hindi-kavita.com/HindiBaba-Bullhe-Bulleh-Shah.php

https://sufinama.org/poets/bulleh-shah/all

Acknowledgements

This book has been a long time in the making and I am grateful to everyone who has been a part of its journey in big and small ways.

I owe special thanks to Prem Nargas whose generous loan of her book started me off on this exploration.

I am grateful to Shreeja Keyal Kanoria for reading the initial set of translations with enthusiasm and for helping me visualise how the book could look by pitching in with a set of preliminary sketches.

I am grateful to Daman Singh for stoically lending her ears to my many cogitations and ruminations on this project over the years.

I am grateful to Dr Anupam Ahluwalia for helping me navigate the Gurmukhi script and pitching in with possible interpretations of Punjabi words and idioms no longer in common use.

I am grateful to Smita Khanna at Jacaranda Literary Agency.

I owe thanks to Bidisha Srivastava at Amaryllis.

And last but not the least, a huge shout out to Danette Gomes for working on the illustrations in this volume in a truly collaborative spirit, both giving and taking creative ideas with openness and alacrity.

www.ingramcontent.com/pod-product-compliance
Lightning Source LLC
Chambersburg PA
CBHW020934180426
43192CB00036B/1148